Be prepared!

PASS
THAT JOB
INTERVIEW

Visit our How To website at www.howto.co.uk

At **www.howto.co.uk** you can engage in conversation with our authors – all of whom have 'been there and done that' in their specialist fields. You can get access to special offers and additional content but most importantly you will be able to engage with, and become a part of, a wide and growing community of people just like yourself.

At **www.howto.co.uk** you'll be able to talk and share tips with people who have similar interests and are facing similar challenges in their lives. People who, just like you, have the desire to change their lives for the better – be it through moving to a new country, starting a new business, growing your own vegetables, or writing a novel.

At **www.howto.co.uk** you'll find the support and encouragement you need to help make your aspirations a reality.

How To Books strives to present authentic, inspiring, practical information in their books. Now, when you buy a title from **How To Books**, you get even more than just words on a page.

Be prepared!

PASS
REVISED and UPDATED
FOURTH EDITION

THAT JOB
INTERVIEW

*"...succeeds in its
aim of giving people
the confidence to
do well at an
interview."*
NEWSCHECK

JULIE-A

howtobooks

Published by How To Books Ltd,
Spring Hill House, Spring Hill Road, Begbroke,
Oxford OX5 1RX. United Kingdom.
Tel: (01865) 375794. Fax: (01865) 379162
info@howtobooks.co.uk
www.howtobooks.co.uk

How To Books greatly reduce the carbon footprint of their books
by sourcing their typesetting and printing in the UK.

First edition 2002
Second edition 2004
Third edition 2008
Reprinted 2008
Fourth edition 2009

British Library Cataloguing in Publication Data.
A catalogue record for this book is available from the British Library.

978 1 84528 354 4

Produced for How To Books by Deer Park Productions, Tavistock
Typeset by Kestrel Data, Exeter
Cover design by Baseline Arts Ltd, Oxford
Printed and bound by the Cromwell Press Group, Trowbridge, Wiltshire

Contents

Preface

Job interviews can be daunting. This book will take you through the essentials of preparing for a successful interview. Whether it is your first interview, or your first in a long time – or even if you are an 'old hand' – you will find tips and hints for success.

Interviews can be some of the most stressful situations we have to face. From the moment you enter the potential employer's building to the time you are back outside, you are on show – and preparing to give a good performance is what can guarantee success. You *can* tip the scales in your favour, with a little work beforehand.

Julie-Ann Amos

Chapter 1

Preparing for Interviews

Preparing for interviews starts before you even know you have an interview.

In this Chapter:

- **the purpose of interviews**
- **preparation**
- **getting your paperwork in order**
- **researching the company**
- **researching yourself**
- **getting from your front door to the interview.**

You can start your preparation before you even know you've been invited to an interview. Understanding the purpose of interviews, and being aware of the contents of your own curriculum vitae or application form is the first step of essential preparation for any interview.

You will need to assemble your job application paperwork carefully and put it in order so you can respond to short-notice invitations to attend interviews. Job hunting isn't easy and you may be surprised at the amount of organisation it takes.

For example, you may need to assemble facts and figures about your salary history and financial requirements, etc. Once invited to an interview, you will also need to assemble some information on the company that's interviewing you, but of course there's no point in preparing detailed information on companies until you know you've got an interview with them.

Is this you?

♦ Surely you can't prepare much for interviews, apart from getting basic information on the company that's going to interview you?

♦ Look, I know who I am and what jobs I've done. I don't need to memorise my own CV – I was there!

♦ I spend ages preparing and getting organised, but it's all wasted when I don't get an interview.

♦ I've sent off so many job applications that I can't remember who's who. It's all a bit of a mess, really.

The purpose of interviews

There's more than one type of interview – nowadays, interviews take many different forms (as we shall see) so that being aware of the different types of interview you may encounter can be very helpful. The How To book *Handling Tough Job Interviews*, also by Julie-Ann Amos, is very helpful in this regard but here are some of the main types.

Recruitment agency interviews

Recruitment agencies exist to place people in jobs. They make their money from the employer – the recruiter – and not from you. Therefore, the common assumption that recruitment agencies are there to help you may be a slight misconception.

Good agencies can be extremely helpful in looking after job hunters properly, by giving them help and support, and placing them in the right job. Others are purely serving the employment needs of the companies and organisations that pay their fees. They may be less concerned with meeting your own individual wants and needs, and more concerned with placing you in a job – any job – that will earn them a fee.

So recruitment agency interviews can be beneficial, as they will give you an opportunity to check out the agency and the way it operates. In an ideal world, the recruitment agency interview should be no more than a means of letting your agency know exactly what you want in a job – so it can tailor any applications it makes on your behalf specifically to your needs. Be aware of the way some agencies operate, however, and watch out for any attempt to 'sell you' a job that isn't in line with your requirements.

With a good agency, an interview can give you tips and advice on presenting yourself well, information on your strong and weaker points, and advice on how to conduct yourself in interviews with potential employers.

Employer interviews

Employer interviews are designed to allow the employer to assess whether or not you are a good fit with their requirements. Usually, a first interview is very much a screening interview, with a second interview being held later for those candidates who pass this initial screening. Your performance at the first interview should therefore really be a matter of being seen to be right for the job. Later interviews are where you would prove yourself to be the *best* candidate.

Personnel or Human Resources (HR) interviews

You will often encounter personnel or HR interviews, as most larger companies insist on them as part of the recruitment process. These interviews are sometimes viewed as 'easy', as HR interviewers rarely ask very technical questions about your specific skills – as they are HR specialists and not usually business managers. Questions are far more likely to revolve around other, more personal areas. But these interviews are not to be underestimated – HR specialists are often very highly trained and experienced in interviewing, and they usually carry out interviews on a regular basis. They are therefore skilled at getting information from you, so be careful – never attempt to pull the wool over their eyes.

Not all interviews are alike – be aware of the purpose of an interview, and this will help you do well in all circumstances.

Preparation

Getting prepared is really what the whole of this book is about. So what exactly is it that you have to prepare? The first two chapters of the book focus on things you can *do* before the interview, and the rest of the book details information you can consider and think over before the interview as a means of preparing yourself for it.

Here are some examples of what you should prepare, ready for a round of potential interviews.

Paperwork

This includes your CV, a copy of the relevant application form, and all documents relating to a particular interview. Have copies of everything to hand well in advance – don't rely on technology (which can let you down) to print copies for you at the last minute.

Your 'shopping list'

Too many people attend interviews with no clear idea of exactly what they want and need from them. Make sure you know what you do and don't want in terms of salary, environment, benefits, role etc.

Research

Make sure you have ready access to any research about the job, the company or organisation you have undertaken previously (see later). It may help you ask questions at interview or help you identify areas you need to clarify to see if this job opportunity meets your wants and needs list – your 'shopping list'.

What you will wear and take

All too often people leave these decisions until the last moment, rushing round looking for the right outfit on interview day. If you can, have your interview outfit cleaned in advance and ready to wear at short notice.

Transport

You need to research and plan the means of transport you intend to use to get to and from the interview. Thinking ahead will allow you to avoid running the risk of being late.

Things to think about

In addition, you will need to think about:

♦ how you will introduce yourself

♦ how to stay calm and relaxed, in what is for most people a stressful situation

♦ how to deal with the interviewer's questions

♦ preparing some sample answers to likely questions

- ◆ your body language, and how to establish a good rapport with your interviewer

- ◆ how to leave the interview gracefully and on a good note.

There are two stages to preparation – physically preparing, and mentally/academically thinking through the interview and potential difficulties you may encounter when you are interviewed.

Getting your paperwork in order

You need to make and have to hand copies of all your essential paperwork relating to the interviewer. You will need a copy of your CV, a copy of any job applications you send off, and the job adverts you are responding to. Of course, all this paperwork can be daunting and expensive to photocopy if you don't have access to a copier – and it can be hard to manage.

Be organised

Consider some sort of filing system. A cheap solution is a simple file or ring binder, in which you can collate job adverts and information by filing them, cutting out job adverts and sticking them onto A4 sheets of paper as necessary. This is important – if you get an interview, you need to be able to read what you have available on the job and the company, and you need to check **exactly** what the employer is looking for, so you can tailor your thinking and preparation to giving a good performance for a particular job interview.

The filing system you use isn't important – what is important is that if anyone calls you to arrange an interview, you can find the information you need easily so you can prepare properly. You don't want to be getting stressed and anxious looking for the job advert in a pile of papers – you need to be calm and to prepare your thoughts carefully if you want to do well at the interview.

Job adverts

Job adverts usually give you a good idea of the skills and abilities the employer is looking for, so you need to read the job advert carefully if you are to prepare properly for an interview. If you are applying for a lot of jobs from adverts, you will need to be very organised, and to keep copies of all the adverts you reply to.

Application forms or packs

You will also need to consider application forms. If you have applied for jobs which involve filling out application forms, ideally you should keep a copy of the form you complete. You don't need to keep a copy of your basic details such as education, job history etc, as this is information that will be on your CV. But you do need to keep a copy of your answers to questions on the form such as 'Describe how you fit the job description', or 'Outline why you feel you are right for this role'. Your responses to questions like these may well be discussed at interview, so you really need to read through what you said on the form before going to the interview.

It's very useful that when an application form is sent to you, it will usually be part of a 'candidate pack', that will give you information such as a job description, structure of the company department, etc. This is all good stuff that will help you to prepare for your interview. Again, it needs to be filed so you can find it when you need it – there's no worse way of preparing for an interview than having to conduct a last-minute paper chase!

You have a lot of resources available to help you prepare for interviews, but keeping them all organised and easily to hand can be almost as stressful as the interview itself!

Researching the company

Application or candidate packs

As mentioned above, when you get an application form, it will often be part of an application pack or candidate pack produced by the organisation. These packs can sometimes be very scrappy and hastily put together, but many of them are very well-presented and give you incredibly useful information about:

♦ what exactly the employer is looking for

♦ whether the employer's requirements are essential or desirable

- how the employer will test whether or not you fit a particular requirement

- special skills and abilities required by the employer

- information on working conditions at the workplace

- information about the organisation

- organisation charts setting out company/ departmental structures

- background to the department and/or the job

- details of salary and benefits, etc

- the recruitment process, and timescales relating to the process.

These packs can be the single most useful thing you have available to you for interview preparation, so keep them safe and read them carefully before the interview. They can help you understand how to present yourself in the best possible light, and give you ideas for questions to raise and points to clarify with the interviewer. Most importantly, they can give you a real feel for the job and the company they describe, which can be very useful in helping you decide whether or not the job is really for you.

If the company doesn't send you a pack, be proactive – call them and ask them for one. If you are invited to an interview, ask them to send you any information on the company they may have. Often companies send out a letter confirming an interview, and/or directions, so when they do, ask them to send you their company literature. If you don't ask, you don't get!

Other sources of company information

Even if you aren't sent an application pack, you can still obtain useful and relevant company information prior to your interview. You can research companies through media such as the internet, reference libraries and papers/journals, for example. Look for any material that will lead to increasing your knowledge of the company.

It is absolutely crucial you understand the culture and environment of the company by whom you will be interviewed, so that you can make the right decision as to whether you would be happy working for them. Research the organisation's history, its current market situation, clients, competitors etc.

The company website

Websites can give you a wealth of information about companies. If you don't know the address of a company's website, look it up by using one of the major research engines such as Yahoo! or Google.

Other internet websites

Here are some other good internet website sources of business information (correct at the time of printing).

www.prnewswire.co.uk
This is a European news network that covers press

releases and features. Allows searching for press releases by company name.

http://news.bbc.co.uk/hi/english/business/companies
This is the BBC news service that will give you all the latest news on companies.

www.thetimes.co.uk
You need to register to use this, but registration is currently free. There are selected news stories, from the latest editions of the two papers. You can search the archive back to January '96.

www.digitallook.com/dlmedia/news/company_news?
Another site with live company news feed, but not easy to search as for example the BBC website.

Libraries

The reference section of your local library may have useful business directories such as Kompass, Dunn & Bradstreet and Kellys.

Papers/journals

Trade magazines are another useful source of company information.

> Application packs are fantastic resources for interview preparation. Always ask for application packs where possible.

Researching yourself

Is this the job you really want?

As you have just read, application packs can help you decide whether or not a job is right for you. An essential part of your interview preparation should always be to evaluate your own needs, wants and desires. If you assess carefully how badly you want this particular job, you will approach the interview with the right mindset.

If you don't really feel the job is ideal for you, but that it's one you could settle for, you can approach the interview more as a means for giving you interview experience. But if the job is the one you really want – that elusive 'dream job' – then the interview becomes extremely important, and you will need to put all your effort into excelling at it.

Know your facts

You may be asked in detail at interview about your salary and benefits expectations. Make sure you know what these are, as you may look rather foolish if you don't. Check out your hourly, weekly or monthly rate (however you are paid) and when you last had a pay rise. Know what benefits you get. If you don't know what you're paid at the moment, you will weaken your negotiating power.

Know what you want

Look at the job, and before you go into the interview decide the minimum salary or pay you would accept, should you be offered it. The job advert may list a salary or salary range, but a company may sometimes pay more for the right person, so always do your homework and decide on your minimum requirements.

When deciding your minimum requirements, you need to factor in additional costs. For example, if you will have a longer journey, your travelling expenses may be higher than you currently pay. Factor in extra costs like this to your requirements, so you can define:

♦ your ideal salary

♦ your minimum acceptable salary – your 'bottom line'.

It is absolutely essential that you know your absolute bottom line, so if you are offered a salary below this, you will know you need to decline the job offer.

Research salary requirements

Employers are very often open to a well-argued justification for a salary offer. If you have done your homework, and are able to show this by justifying your salary requirements, they are much more likely to be met.

You can do this by looking at other adverts for similar jobs, or talking to people you know in similar jobs, etc. People who can produce evidence that they have researched their requirements are far more likely to get them accepted.

Take some credentials

Don't go overboard, but if it is appropriate take
to the interview some work you have done – drawings
you have done, or papers, reports you have written,
etc.

Research how badly you want the job, your
current position and needs, and your salary
requirements. Knowing the facts and doing the
necessary research will almost always pay
dividends.

Getting from your front door to the interview

One area you need to prepare in advance is how you
will actually get to the interview. You need to check
out, well in advance, both *how* you will get there –
bus, taxi, car, train – and *how long* this is likely to take.

Be on time

Being late for interviews isn't necessarily the end of
the world – a pleasant apology and good excuse can
prevent problems – but if an interviewer is working to
a schedule, you may end up not being able to have a
proper interview. Candidates turning up 30 minutes
late for a 45-minute interview place the interviewer in
a dilemma – do they give you a 30-minute interview
and 'steal' 15 minutes from their next candidate? That
isn't fair! Or do they only give you 15 minutes, which
more or less means you won't stand a chance! Don't
put them in that position – be on time.

Check schedules

Don't just plan to get a bus or train – actually check the departure and arrival times. Changes in schedule, repairs, etc can all stop scheduled services from running to plan. Check for last-minute updates, by using facilities such as train websites, AA Roadwatch on teletext, etc.

Be prepared for an emergency

Take a mobile phone, or change for the telephone with you – that way you can call ahead in an emergency, or if you are delayed.

Be generous

Be generous with your time. Delays, breakdowns, traffic, missed trains/buses, etc – all are reasonable, but at the same time avoidable excuses for being late. Allow sufficient time to get to the interview early, then find somewhere nearby to wait in comfort, so you can relax. Nothing makes people more stressed than a rushed journey, getting to the interview late or with seconds to spare. Plan to get there early and wait around – you can always use the time to prepare for your interview further, read through any notes, etc.

Plan your journey carefully, and allow extra time for unforeseen circumstances. Emergencies may be understandable, but getting there late can still mean you don't get a proper interview.

Summary points

♦ Understand the purpose of interviews, so you can structure your preparation accordingly.

♦ Prepare all the necessary information – if you don't need to use it, at least you had it ready.

♦ Get all your paperwork ready – organise it so you can easily find the information you need.

♦ Research the company interviewing you so you can ask them sensible questions and resolve any queries you may have.

♦ Research your own wants and needs – and be prepared to justify them if necessary.

♦ Plan your journey with military precision, so everything goes smoothly on the day.

Chapter 2

Presentation

Presentation is your window-dressing – the shop front you display to the world. A good display attracts more customers and makes them more likely to buy!

In this Chapter:

♦ **making a good impression**
♦ **what to wear**
♦ **personal presentation**
♦ **waiting.**

The best candidate can let themselves down and even lose a job at interview by being poorly presented. We all know it's wrong to judge by appearances, but let's face it, you also have to take human nature into account – people do. Before interviewing you, an interviewer will have made themselves look presentable, arranged a room, refreshments, read your CV, and prepared questions to ask you. In return, it is perfectly natural (and not unreasonable) for them to expect you to have made some effort yourself.

Presentation is all about appearances. A poor candidate can look good and make a decent impression by looking as though they have researched and prepared thoroughly for the interview, so impressions count.

But presentation is about more than just your appearance – anyone can make the effort to look good without buying new clothes. It's about letting the interviewer know you have tried – that you care about making a good impression, and that you take the interview seriously enough to prepare.

Is this you?

♦ People shouldn't judge by appearances. I should get the job based on what I can do, not what I look like.

♦ If I dress up for an interview, it looks too keen. I prefer to look as if I've just come from a normal day at work.

♦ Why bother? All the interviews I've had have been with people who didn't make any effort to look smart themselves!

♦ If I look too smart, everyone at work will know where I'm going – it's a bit of a give-away!

Making a good impression

Making a good impression isn't just about the clothes you wear. It's about the whole impression you give at interview. Everyone tends to focus on first impressions, and it's often said that interviewers decide within 30 seconds of meeting you whether or not they want you. Some judgements are made on a conscious level within this short timeframe, it's true, and certainly we are all subconsciously influenced by first impressions to some extent.

So what goes into this impression? It's a mixture of factors, some of which you can influence, and some you can't:

♦ physical appearance

♦ dress

♦ manner – are you friendly, relaxed and approachable?

♦ what you say

♦ how you behave

♦ neatness

♦ timekeeping

♦ attitude – enthusiastic, shy, etc

♦ personal hygiene and grooming.

Most of these factors are subjective, not objective – that is, they cannot be measured, although some of them have at least some common standard. For example, although 'smart dress' is subjective, most people have a fairly clear idea of what they would agree is smart dress. Other factors such as physical appearance are very subjective indeed.

Given that, generally speaking, presentation is based on impressions that are subjective, just how can you prepare and make sure you present yourself well in all situations? You can't – not in all situations. You might turn yourself out spotlessly for interview to find that the company has a relaxed dress policy, for example, and everyone else is in jeans and shirts. What you can do is try your best to achieve a happy medium, so that you will do well in the majority of situations.

> Presentation is based on appearance, which is often in the eye of the beholder.

What to wear

Smart dress

What is meant by 'smart dress' is subjective. Be relatively conservative, and opt for something businesslike and appropriate to the situation – obviously some jobs or fields require different styles or standards of dress.

Pay attention to detail

Details such as odd or missing buttons, socks that don't match, torn clothing, frayed edges or loose ends all detract from your image. Check your clothes carefully before you put them on.

Colour

Choose a businesslike colour. Daffodil yellow may be your favourite colour, but a more neutral shirt or blouse will probably go down better at interview. Splashes of colour, such as a colourful blouse or tie, can be stylish and they may make you more memorable and well-presented, but don't go too far. Save the more exotic components of your wardrobe for *after* you've got the job!

Shoes

Make sure that shoes are not scuffed or dirty, and that they go with the rest of your outfit. Beware of new shoes – it is easy to forget to remove those white labels from the bottom of new shoes – not a serious mistake, but someone might see them and that's not what you want to be remembered for.

Personal comfort

Never underestimate personal comfort. Looking perfect at the price of your personal comfort rarely serves any purpose. Your discomfort may show without you realising it, especially in the case of shoes that pinch or rub. Wearing something comfortable will make you more relaxed and less stressed, and will allow you to behave more naturally.

> Deciding what to wear isn't actually that difficult. But don't leave things to chance – plan in advance and check all items carefully.

Personal presentation

Hygiene

There is more to presenting a good image than what you wear. Interviews can often be in fairly small rooms, so things like hygiene, body odour, bad breath, etc, *will* be noticed.

Perfume/aftershave

Beware of wearing too strong a perfume or aftershave. It can be overpowering in a small room, or it may be not to the interviewer's liking. At the very least, it's unnecessary. Wear something subtle, not strong.

Grooming

Basic details like having a hair cut if necessary, washing your hair, clean fingernails, etc, shouldn't need mentioning, but it's surprising how many candidates forget to check these little details and turn up for interviews with chipped nail polish, food on their moustache, or hair that obviously hasn't been brushed or combed! Do make sure you build in enough time for a quick last minute check in the mirror before your interview begins!

Shoes and bags

Shoes and bags are easily overlooked as well. Many candidates dressed to perfection let themselves down with old or scuffed shoes, or simply wear shoes that obviously have no idea what polish is! Bags can also be old and tired – and battered briefcases don't impress anyone by looking well used; they just look scruffy. Remember the details.

> There is more to how you look than your clothes. Your appearance can be enhanced by good dress, but no amount of smart dressing can cover up a basic hygiene or grooming problem.

Waiting

As we have said previously, plan to get there early and wait. Waiting can be more complex than you think, however.

Where to wait

Bear in mind that there may be nowhere nearby to wait. Not all businesses are conveniently situated near shops and cafés, and you may have to wait at a location ten or fifteen minutes' walk away if you want to wait in a coffee bar or café. Or you could try waiting in other places such as a local library. Ideally, you should avoid waiting at the place of the interview. Try to arrive early enough to find somewhere else to wait – somewhere you can relax and feel calm and do some last minute preparation if necessary.

Don't wait in a smoking area, or smoke immediately before your interview – some people are sensitive to cigarette smoke, and dislike it. Going into an interview smelling of cigarette smoke may be unpleasant for interviewers, particularly if the interview takes place in a small room.

If you do have to wait at the place of the interview, for example if the weather is particularly bad, or the building is in a remote location or on an industrial estate, now is the time to be nice to the receptionist! Ideally, you want to be allowed to wait, but not be announced until the correct time. Interviewers may not be impressed by interviewees who are too early – it may create the impression that you are desperate to impress.

Ask the receptionist pleasantly if there is somewhere you can wait, but say that you would prefer not to be announced until at most five minutes before your interview time. When you are ready, don't forget to remind the receptionist that you are ready – you don't want to be forgotten and make the interviewer think you're late!

Eating and drinking whilst waiting

As we said above, many interview rooms can be quite small, and not everyone likes cigarette smoke. So, if you have a quick cigarette just before the interview to calm your nerves, have it in a well ventilated place and make sure your breath is fresh afterwards!

If you are having a coffee, tea or soft drink while you wait, beware of drinking too much – an interview can often last an hour, more if there is more than one person to see. You don't want to have to visit the loo halfway through! Coffee also contains chemicals that can add to your nervousness.

Beware of alcohol. A quick drink may be ideal for relaxing you or calming your nerves, but it may lead to over-confidence, and alcohol on the breath is rarely appreciated at any interview. The smell can also linger on your clothes, as with cigarettes.

Try to avoid either eating just before an interview, or being interviewed on an empty stomach. Either may cause embarrassment, particularly if your stomach starts to make noises during the interview.

Prepare to wait

Take with you your notes, a copy of the job advert, and any other relevant literature you have and have a last-minute read through everything, so it is fresh in your mind.

Arriving early only to hang about is pointless. Plan to use waiting time to maximum effectiveness. Being busy while you wait will reduce your stress levels.

Summary points

♦ **Making a good impression is about more than the way you look.**

♦ **Choose your interview clothes and accessories carefully. It's not a fashion parade – it's about creating the right image and impression.**

- Don't ignore your personal presentation.

- Plan your journey to the interview with military precision, allowing for contingencies and waiting time.

- Hanging about isn't waiting. Waiting is a slot of time you can use effectively to calm and prepare yourself.

Chapter 3

Meeting and Greeting

First impressions count – there's no denying it. But they can also be changed and influenced.

In this Chapter:

♦ **arriving**
♦ **breaking the ice**
♦ **shaking hands**
♦ **accepting refreshments**
♦ **sitting down.**

There is a common saying that an interviewer decides within the first 30 seconds of meeting you whether or not he/she wants to hire you. This is unlikely to be true, especially now that managers are becoming more and more enlightened, more aware of 'human factors' such as psychology, and are better trained in interviewing techniques, etc.

However, there is no denying the fact that preconceptions and prejudices exist, as do instant reactions. People do tend to react positively or negatively to others quite quickly; to get around this at interview you have to bear in mind that you *can* influence interviewers, even to the extent of changing an initial negative reaction. Obviously, the quicker you start to influence them, the better, so the early stages of an interview are vital, when you are introducing yourself, meeting and greeting, etc.

Some people make their minds up less quickly, and are initially objective, forming their opinion of you over a longer period of time. Again, influencing them early on helps them to make the right decision about you.

Is this you?

♦ I hate it when you can see that people have prejudged you. It's not fair!

♦ This is a big deal for just getting into a room with someone – it seems over-complicated.

♦ The beginning is just when I'm *most* nervous. I don't need all these extra things to worry about.

♦ The whole meeting and greeting thing is a con trick. Let's face it, they're just trying to lull you into a false sense of security for the grilling that's to come.

Arriving

From the moment you enter . . .

You're on show right from the start:

- You may be on security camera from the moment you enter the building

- Receptionists/PAs, etc, may be asked their opinion, or what they thought of you, so be on your best behaviour with everybody from the moment you step into the building.

Remember what people look for

- People like people who are like themselves

- People like people who can initiate conversation if necessary

- People like others to respond if they initiate conversation

- People like people with confidence (but not too much!)

- People relate to people who can express themselves appropriately

Bags, coats and other baggage

- Try to avoid carrying too much baggage

- Ladies should avoid carrying both a handbag and briefcase – it's too much

- If possible, avoid carrying multiple items such as a coat and umbrella *and* briefcase into the interview

- Ask if you can leave things in reception before you are announced – it shows confidence as well as getting rid of the clutter!

- Discard or put away newspapers, etc before arriving

- If you have a file of interview information, by all
  means carry it so they will know you have gone to
  the time and trouble of preparing, but don't be too
  obvious about it – understated is best.

> Arriving is important – it's part of those vital first
> few seconds.

Breaking the ice

Start the ball rolling

Never be afraid to initiate conversation if necessary. It
shows confidence without being pushy. Safe comments
are things like 'It's a beautiful day, isn't it?' or 'What
a lovely building; have you been here long?'

Respond appropriately

If a conversation is started, don't rush in too quickly.
'Small talk' is an appropriate phrase – most
interviewers start off with a few quick and easy
questions and comments to get people relaxed and
comfortable. So don't give a great long explanation to
a question at this stage. Keep your answers short, to
the point, and positive.

Beware of negatives

Even if you have had the journey from hell to get to
your interview, play things down if asked about it.
Starting off on a negative footing isn't really ideal. It

may not do you any harm, but it is unlikely to do you any good either. Journey and travel details are often a potential pitfall. Remember, if you get the job they will be expecting you to travel to work every day, on time. So giving the information that the journey was long or difficult isn't giving them the impression it would be easy for you to work for them! If you need to explain lateness, for example, end with a positive note, such as 'The journey coming from my current place of work was a nightmare – obviously coming here from home would be much easier.'

Body language

With body language, three things seem to make people relate to each other quickly and easily at a first meeting:

♦ Make eye contact – look them in the eye

♦ Smile – to show you are pleased to see them

♦ The 'eyebrow flash' – quickly raising your eyebrows when being introduced apparently shows interest in the other person and indicates a willingness to establish a good relationship.

The first few seconds of being introduced are actually a good opportunity to get things off on the right foot.

Shaking hands

Don't panic!

People very often dread shaking hands, and yet it's a minor thing that is usually over in a second or two. It's hard to see why people are so nervous about it. It does, however, give an important element to the impression you make in those vital first few minutes.

Sweaty palms

You may have sweaty palms. At worst, this can be obvious and unpleasant. On the other hand, it may not even be consciously noticed by the interviewer, but subconsciously you could be transmitting a signal that you are nervous. Very discreetly and without being noticed, wipe your hand before shaking your interviewer's hand. For example, you could rest your right hand on your leg when waiting, and as you stand up or step forward to shake, just run your palm over your clothes. Never be seen to wipe your hand before shaking – it shows you feel dirty and unworthy to touch them – it's very subordinate. Conversely, *never* wipe your hand after shaking someone else's – it shows you didn't like touching the other person!

The 'dead fish'

A limp handshake is sometimes known as the 'dead fish'. We've all at sometime shaken someone's hand and it's been floppy and lifeless. Feels awful, doesn't it? Don't fall into this trap yourself – hold your interviewer's hand firmly. Limp handshakes come across as unconfident. This type of handshake says:

♦ I'm not confident

♦ I don't have any character

♦ I'm not comfortable shaking hands

♦ I'm nervous.

The 'death grip'

On the other hand, don't grip someone's hand too strongly. People resent it, and it has become something of a stereotype, and may be seen as the action of an aggressive business person. It's true that some employers *want* a firm handshake, especially for sales-type roles, if they're looking for a strong character. But tread carefully – be guided by your interviewer. If your interviewer gives you a 'death grip', responding in kind will probably be the right thing to do. Too-firm handshakes, however, are definitely inappropriate for older (ie, elderly) interviewers, and some ladies – they can hurt. And if you are shaking hands with someone who's your equal, it becomes a competitive gesture. Be sensible about how strong your handshake grip is – the 'death grip' handshake says:

♦ I'm overconfident

♦ I'm competitive

♦ I'm insensitive

- I'm pushy

- I'm trying to dominate

- I'm trying to force my ideas

- I'm trying to give you a message.

The perfect handshake

- Engage the whole hand, palm to palm.

- Match the hand pressure of the other person. If they are a person with a firm handshake, you want to shake back just as firmly. For people with a weaker handshake you should soften your handshake grip in return.

- It shouldn't last longer than how long it takes to say 'One, two, three.'

- Accompany the handshake with a smile and eye contact.

> Shaking hands takes no more than a second or two, but it all adds to the interviewer's impression of you.

Accepting refreshments

The golden rule

The golden rule is to be comfortable, so that you can relax. So if you are desperately thirsty, of course you should accept refreshments.

Extreme nerves

If you are so nervous you fear spilling something, politely say 'No, thank you' and decline. Better to do this than to accept in an attempt to co-operate with the interviewer and then have a catastrophe!

Check what your interviewer does

By far the safest option is to ask if the interviewer is having anything. Some people feel embarrassed if they are offered coffee and accept, and then the interviewer doesn't join them. Say something simple such as:

♦ 'I'll join you if you're having something, otherwise I'm fine, thank you.'

♦ 'Only if you're going to.'

♦ 'Are you having anything?'

Smoking and eating

Never eat in an interview, regardless of what the interviewer does. Interviews are about answering the interviewer's questions, and it's hard to talk when you are eating. You end up juggling words and mouthfuls, and it just looks clumsy.

You can see what a disaster area refreshments can be – be careful before accepting.

Sitting down

Wait your turn!

Never sit down before being invited to do so. Waiting is not only polite, it gives a nervous interviewer confidence, and gives them the lead.

Be alert and interested

The aim in an interview is to appear alert and interested. You can't do this if you are slumped. Lean slightly forward – not too much or you will look odd! Sit up straight.

Stay relaxed

Stay relaxed but not slumped. Sitting uncomfortably and bolt upright may look great at first, but after 30 minutes it may be so uncomfortable that your whole body language changes – the interviewer isn't a mindreader and he/she may decide you aren't happy with the job or the company if you *look* unhappy.

Do something with your hands

Oddly enough, when sitting down, one of the hardest things to do is to decide what to do with your hands! Don't dangle them off the arms of the chair – it's odd. And don't clutch them together, which looks nervous. Find a relaxed way of holding them or laying them on your legs.

Territory and positioning

You may get to choose where to sit, or the interviewer may direct you to a seat. This positioning is rarely random – so choose your territory carefully. Don't sit facing a bright light, or with the sun in your eyes. If possible don't sit directly opposite the interviewer face-to-face, looking directly at each other – it's confrontational and may make some interviewers feel uncomfortable. Try to sit at an angle to them if at all possible. You can easily do this by moving your chair very slightly as you sit down, so you are positioned at a slight angle to them.

Avoid closed body language

Avoid folding your arms and crossing your legs – closing your body language. It says you are unreceptive and not willing to listen.

> How you sit says a lot to the interviewer, and subconsciously it will be adding to their opinion of you.

Summary points

♦ Remember you may be noticed from the second you enter the building.

♦ Breaking the ice may be something you have to initiate.

♦ Shaking hands appropriately takes only a few seconds but adds to the image you are presenting.

♦ Accept refreshments where necessary and/or appropriate.

♦ Even something as simple as the way in which you sit down can convey a message to the interviewer.

Chapter 4

Handling Nerves

Being nervous isn't just a rotten feeling to have to experience — it can ruin your chances of giving your best performance as well!

In this Chapter:

- **handling emotions**
- **transforming thought processes**
- **relaxing and calming yourself**
- **emergency measures.**

Being nervous can be a pretty unpleasant feeling. Nobody likes to feel anxious, under-confident, fearful of the situation, unsure of themselves — but most people have experienced one or more of these feelings at some time or other.

But the risk of feeling bad isn't the only problem. Uncontrolled nervousness can alter your behaviour, your body language and what you say — when you feel nervous you can behave differently to how you usually behave. And interviews are doubly difficult because both you and the interviewer may be nervous.

Controlling your nerves isn't easy, and even if it were, it's one more thing to have to think about in what is an inherently stressful situation. But keeping your anxiety under control can reap huge benefits and nerves *can* be controlled, so it is worth trying. Learning simple techniques will at first help, and eventually may even become an unconscious habit, so you automatically control your nerves better with practice.

Is this you?

♦ I hate interviews. I never do well, and I never will. What's the point?

♦ I don't believe you can ever really control nerves – some people are just more nervous than others and that's that.

♦ It's all right for interviewers – they don't get nervous.

♦ If I spend all my time controlling my nerves, how will I be able to concentrate on the interview itself and on doing myself justice?

Handling emotions

Thoughts versus emotions

With nerves, is it really your emotions that are a problem? In many ways, the problem is more often a thought process than an actual emotion. Let me explain: thoughts and emotions are not the same. For example:

THOUGHT	EMOTION GENERATED
'This is a scary situation'	Fear
'I might not get the job'	Nervousness or anxiety
'Damn, I messed that up!'	Hopelessness
'I should have said X instead . . .'	Frustration

Controlling emotions

As you can see, it is actually thoughts that generate emotions. Someone who feels fear, anxiety, nervousness, hopelessness, frustration, etc, would find it very difficult to do anything about it – and that's perfectly natural. But just how do you *stop* being afraid?

The problem is that once the emotion is there, it's happening, and very hard to stop. Often these emotions produce complex hormonal or chemical reactions in the body, and controlling reactions is next to impossible. The key to controlling any emotion – such as nervousness, for example – is to remember that it is caused by a thought process. Disrupt the thought process and you cut off the stimulus that causes the emotion.

Thoughts and emotions are not the same at all.
You can influence your thoughts, but your
emotions are a reaction to them.

Transforming thought processes

Internal dialogue

For nervousness, you need to identify the thought
process behind your nervousness and so deal with it
more positively. You do this by internal dialogue.
Discuss the thought process with yourself, and try just
focusing on the thoughts – that will take your
attention away from the emotion and its biological
effects on your system. Don't worry that you won't
have time for this – conducting internal dialogue is
pretty quick for most people; these split-second
'conversations' usually go on in our heads all the time.

Identify thought processes

♦ Identify the thought process, eg, 'I might not get
  the job.'

♦ Doing this takes your mind off the emotion you are
  feeling.

♦ It also refocuses your attention.

Evaluate rationally

♦ Evaluate the thought *rationally* – this means
  examining it unemotionally.

- Is it justified to that extent?

- Is it even true?

- Would the consequences that you fear really be all that bad?

- Talk it over with yourself – *rationally*, eg, 'They wouldn't have interviewed me if they didn't think I was a possibility. If I don't get it, there are other jobs out there. But I might get it – who knows?'

Replace the negative thought with something more helpful

- amend it

- replace with a more sensible, appropriate and/or positive thought, eg, 'I might get the job or I might not. Either way this is valuable experience I can learn from.'

Re-examine how you feel

- Re-examine the emotion you feel

- It should either be reducing or gone, eg, 'Hey! If I see it as a learning experience, this interview doesn't make me feel quite so nervous!'

Amending the thought processes behind emotions helps us to control unwanted emotions such as nervousness.

Relaxing and calming yourself

Breathe

♦ Getting oxygen to your brain will make you able to think more clearly.

♦ Breathe deeply and slowly.

♦ Try breathing in for a count of five, then out for a count of five.

♦ Get some fresh air. Like breathing, this will increase the supply of oxygen to your brain and make you able to think better.

♦ Take a short walk – for the same reason.

Calming rituals

♦ People often have calming rituals, such as having a cup of tea. If you don't have one, establish one!

♦ Have a drink – preferably a soft drink, juice or water.

♦ Remember that tea and coffee are stimulants, so if you are very nervous, they won't help and could even make things worse – caffeine can make you feel even more anxious!

Relaxing yourself

♦ Find somewhere to sit down.

♦ Concentrate on relaxing.

- Starting with your feet and moving up, tighten each part of your body in turn and then relax it. This will remove any muscle tension.

- Concentrate on relaxing your body – stop nervous, edgy movements and actions such as fiddling, licking your lips, biting lips, tapping feet, etc.

> Relaxing and calming yourself is something you need to do physically. Just the act of physically concentrating on changing things helps your mind focus on something constructive and positive, and will reduce nervousness.

Emergency measures

Keep things in proportion

- You are not alone. Everyone dries up at some stage.

- Sometimes the physical effects of anxiety can affect the vocal chords and make it hard to speak. Or you get so nervous you don't know *what* to say.

- Panicking will only make things worse.

Buy yourself some time

- Ask for a glass of water.

- Not only will the water help, but the time it takes to get it for you will buy you some breathing space so you can collect your thoughts.

♦ Use this to try to relax.

♦ Pause in your conversation, or when asked a question. Count to five then continue. This doesn't sound as odd as you might think – pausing to gather your thoughts is a natural thing, and people often do it.

♦ Ask for thinking time. You can always say 'Can I have a minute to think this one through?'

♦ If you're asked a difficult question, ask if you can come back to it. It's not ideal, but can be acceptable. For example, you might say, 'Sorry, can we come back to that question in a few minutes?'

Refocus on something else

♦ Stop thinking about being nervous, and start thinking about relaxing.

♦ Refocus your attention – use some of the internal dialogue technique we have previously discussed.

Come clean and ask for help

♦ Admit it! Admitting honestly to being nervous can help the interviewer carry out the interview. There is nothing wrong with saying honestly (but not in a grovelling way) something such as 'I'm sorry – I'm actually quite nervous about this interview, as I really like the look of this job.' Giving a positive reason for your nervousness will make you seem less like a shrinking violet.

Everyone gets nervous at times. Being able to control this and turn it to your advantage can help your performance greatly, as well as making you feel a whole lot better!

Summary points

♦ Learn that emotions can be handled – they aren't something that you are totally at the mercy of, something you can only suffer until they go away.

♦ The key to handling emotions is to identify and amend the thought processes that underlie them. This is done by internal dialogue.

♦ Learn physical mechanisms that help to relax and calm you – and use them.

♦ Remember that you can cope with an emergency, by resorting to emergency measures.

Chapter 5

Body Language

Body language is a huge subject. Understanding it can make life a lot easier, as it can add greatly to the image you present to an interviewer.

In this Chapter:

♦ **the golden rule**
♦ **gestures and meanings**
♦ **eye contact**
♦ **listening skills**
♦ **mirroring**
♦ **disagreeing.**

Body language is a huge subject upon which many books have been written. Unfortunately, they can sometimes give you conflicting advice, and studying body language in depth can mean you spend all your time studying other people's mannerisms instead of concentrating on your own! You need to have enough information to allow you to focus on performing at your best at interview. Knowing the basics of body language can increase your performance at interview greatly. Being able to control your own body language makes it easier for you to relate to interviewers, and to make a good impression. It can also make you appear more confident, more honest, and more in tune with the interviewer.

But there is one other advantage of knowing about body language – it helps you control your nerves, if you suffer from nervousness. Concentrating on your physical actions will take your attention away from negative thought processes and feeling nervous, and make you focus instead on what you are actually doing. This can reduce your nervousness significantly.

Is this you?

♦ I can't be bothered with body language – I already have a million things to think about in an interview!

♦ Everyone knows about body language now so it's irrelevant. We all know what things mean, so there's no big secret advantage to knowing it any more.

♦ I think all the advice I've ever seen on body language is just false – it just makes people look silly, as if they're acting.

♦ I know the basics and what not to do – but can you really use body language to make an interviewer like you more?

The golden rule

The golden rule with body language is to match your interviewer's body language. Like attracts like.

Match verbal with non-verbal behaviours

♦ Use non-verbal behaviour – ie, body language, to reinforce and back up what you are saying verbally.

♦ Try never to use body language that gives a different message from your verbal message, such as saying 'Yes' and shaking your head at the same time, or a more common example, saying 'No' and nodding.

♦ The trick is to always match non-verbal messages with verbal messages – so you should always nod when you agree, shake your head when you are disagreeing, etc.

Mismatching

So what happens if you mismatch – if you literally do say 'yes' and at the same time shake your head? (Try it – it's actually quite hard to do!) Research varies, but almost every piece of research that has been carried out on the subject shows that the *non-verbal* signal will come through strongest. So the non-verbal signal will be the one believed, and the other person may reject the content of your words, or they will not even notice the words at all, but will end up feeling you've said what your non-verbal signal said!

Other types of matching

There are other ways in which you can use the principle of matching, that like attracts like. These will be explained later, but in particular, a technique called 'mirroring' is useful. This is where you match, or mirror, the other person's body language, which almost always has the effect of making the person you're talking to feel more in rapport with you – they relate to you better.

> Like attracts like. People like people like them. People relate better to people they feel 'in synch' with. This is one of the fundamental aspects of body language.

Gestures and meanings

As we have said, an amazing number of books on body language have been published. Listing the things you can do to convey certain meanings isn't always helpful, as it will give you too much to think about in a situation which we know is inherently stressful.

Instead, here are some of the main impressions you may give to an interviewer, and some of the main signals by which your body language conveys these impressions. Choose which ones to practise and which ones to avoid – that way, you can focus on improving just one area at a time, which won't overload you!

Defensiveness

These actions convey the impression that you have something to hide:

♦ crossing or folding your arms

♦ sitting at too much of an angle to the interviewer, so you have to turn your head to look at him/her

♦ pointing your finger when making a point

♦ using your hand in a 'karate chop' gesture when making a point

♦ looking down when speaking

♦ not making eye contact.

Suspicious and distrusting

These actions suggest you are distrusting:

♦ crossing or folding your arms

♦ looking at your interviewer from underneath your eyebrows

♦ looking at your interviewer sideways – out of the corner of your eye (usually caused by sitting too much at an angle to him/her)

♦ rubbing your eyes

♦ frowning

♦ touching nose or face

♦ rubbing the back of the neck.

Nervousness

All these convey nervousness:

♦ pinching your skin

♦ fidgeting

♦ jiggling the contents of your pockets

♦ running your tongue along the front of your teeth

♦ clearing your throat

♦ running your fingers through your hair

♦ wringing your hands

♦ biting on pens or other objects

♦ twiddling your thumbs

♦ biting your fingernails (both the action itself and evidence of it)

♦ tongue-clicking

♦ gritting your teeth

♦ biting your lips.

Positive body language

All these actions, on the other hand, will enable you to establish a good rapport with interviewer:

♦ good eye contact

♦ leaning forward slightly in your chair

- tilting your head whilst maintaining eye contact with your interviewer

- open-lipped smiling

- open hands with palms visible

- unbuttoning your coat or jacket upon being seated

- keeping your chin up

- putting tips of fingers of one hand against the tips of fingers of other hand in the 'praying' or 'steepling' position

- having your hands joined behind back your when standing.

Body language can be a lot to take in and master. Concentrate on identifying the bad habits and eliminating them, and add a few good ones.

Eye contact

The importance of eye contact

- Eye contact is important as it conveys confidence and trust.

- It establishes a rapport with the other person – ie, a link, a connection or relationship between you.

- When speaking to someone, establishing eye contact allows you to check that they understand and are still interested in what you are saying.

- When listening, establishing eye contact conveys your attention and is a gesture of politeness.

- Lack of eye contact shows evasiveness, and makes it almost impossible to establish rapport with someone.

Eye contact when listening

There are two ways of looking at eye contact – either as a listener or as a speaker. As a listener, you need to make a great deal more eye contact – it's simply more appropriate for a listener to do so, and to extend your eye contact for longer periods of time than if you are speaking.

Eye contact when speaking

On the other hand, if you are a speaker, your listener will end up feeling uncomfortable if you maintain complete eye contact with them for too long. About five to ten seconds of eye contact is about right for making a connection with your listener. After that you should make your eye contact less complete and look away. Otherwise, the connection with your listener becomes too intense, and can start to feel like a staring match. Speakers tend therefore to make and break eye contact regularly, whereas listeners tend to keep eye contact for extended periods of time.

Excessive eye contact

Excessive or inappropriate eye contact will prevent you from establishing a good rapport with your interviewer:

♦ eye contact that is too strong can be too intense

♦ it can become a battle of wills

♦ it can be intimidating

♦ it can be over-familiar

♦ holding eye contact for too long can make the person speaking uncomfortable

♦ it can make you look stupid as a listener (as if you are a zombie drinking in every word!)

♦ glancing away occasionally is perfectly acceptable, so long as you restore contact quickly.

Eye contact is probably the most important element of body language. It can make or break the rapport between people in a very short time.

Listening skills

Active listening

Listening isn't just something you do with your ears! It is something you have to do actively in an interview – you don't just have to listen, you have to be *seen* to be listening. This is active listening. Listening signals or behaviours include:

- making eye contact

- nodding

- making 'listening noises' ('Mmm', 'Uh-huh', etc)

- smiling

- leaning forward

- open body language

- tilting the head to one side

- reacting to what your interviewer is saying.

Concentration

The easiest way to listen properly is purely and simply to concentrate on what the person is saying! This tends to make most people exhibit at least some of the signs of active listening listed above.

Questioning

There are other, non-body language ways you can enhance your listening skills. A good way of either showing you have been listening or checking your understanding is to ask questions. You don't necessarily need to interrupt – wait until they pause or stop, and then off you go; it's your turn. Try 'Can I just check I got that correctly . . . ?'

Reflecting

Reflecting is repeating back what you just heard, in a way that isn't obvious. It checks your understanding is correct, and also shows them you understood. It also means that you are telling them what they just told you – and remember that people like people who are like them – it will add to the matching effect you are trying to create. Here are some reflecting phrases:

- 'So what you're saying is . . . ?'

- 'So you think . . . ?'

- 'Then would you agree that . . . ?'

- I agree. It *is* important that . . .'.

Listening is an active, not passive process. It is a good opportunity to relax and make a good impression at the same time.

Mirroring

What is mirroring?

Mirroring is when you imitate someone else's body language. It is like reflecting, except that reflecting is a means of establishing a rapport with someone verbally, whereas mirroring is its non-verbal equivalent. It is basically copying someone else's body language.

Why mirror?

- people like people like themselves

- it helps you establish a rapport with your interviewer

- it establishes a connection between you and your interviewer

- it strengthens any connection or rapport between you that may already exist.

A word of caution

Mirroring is something that many books on body language refer to. But many attempts at mirroring go badly wrong, as this is a very subtle technique. You need to mirror very carefully and gently, so it isn't at all obvious, otherwise you will look very strange indeed! Remember:

- never mirror aggressive interviewers

- don't mirror nervous people

- don't mirror bad habits like scratching

- only mirror people who themselves have good body language

- don't overdo it! – be very, very, subtle

- if you make it obvious that you are mirroring, you have failed.

Mirroring gestures

Mirroring *gestures* is where many people go wrong – it's simply too obvious. If someone smiles, smiling back is mirroring, but it also looks perfectly natural. But crossing your legs as soon as the other person does can look ludicrous.

♦ Don't mirror immediately – leave a gap of a few
seconds.

♦ Don't mirror exactly – you could mirror crossed
legs by crossing your ankles, for example.

♦ Be subtle – mirror reduced versions of what your
interviewer is doing; For example, you could mirror
their running a hand through their hair by just
brushing back your fringe or tucking your hair
behind one ear.

♦ Remember you don't have to produce an exact
mirror image – if your interviewer leans to the left,
wait a short while then lean either to the left or
right yourself – it is the leaning you are mirroring,
not its precise direction.

Mirroring is very effective for establishing rapport
and contact with the interviewer. Unfortunately,
it is very hard to do subtly, and many people end
up looking foolish.

Disagreeing

Your right to an opinion

Interviewers are in charge during an interview
situation, and it's true that they do control whether or
not you get the job. But that doesn't mean you have to
agree with everything they say – it might curry favour,
but it may be against what you really believe, and may
even make you look weak.

Tell the truth, and if you disagree with something the interviewer says, don't be afraid to say so – nicely! Most people would rather someone stood up for themselves than agreed with everything. Plus, there is always the chance that the interviewer is merely testing you – saying something they *expect* you to disagree with, to see whether or not you have the strength of character to do so.

You may also find that if you agree with them because you think it will look better, later on – in the interview or afterwards – it becomes apparent that you have been 'found out'. It's far better never to be dishonest, and so there *will* be occasions when you need to be true to yourself and disagree with an interviewer.

Question before disagreeing

If you disagree with something your interviewer says, check your understanding first. Ask a question or questions to clarify his/her meaning, before saying you disagree. It is far better to make sure you didn't misunderstand before you put your cards on the table.

Be surprised to disagree

Obviously, some people are concerned about disagreeing with an interviewer, as they don't want to give a bad impression. A good way to counteract this is to show surprise when you disagree – as if you expected to agree with the other person, thus creating an impression of how similar you are – good old matching again! Say you're surprised, and use body language to reinforce what you are saying, by raising your eyebrows and saying, for example:

♦ 'Well, I've always been in favour of . . . myself.'

♦ 'I'm surprised – I actually don't find that myself.'

♦ 'How strange – I found them/it very helpful.'

♦ 'That's interesting, because I haven't found that to be the case.'

Don't lie

Don't fall into the trap of lying and agreeing for the sake of it. If you get found out, you will have shown yourself to be dishonest, and that is one thing interviewers hate!

Disagree graciously

One reason why people don't want to disagree with things that are said to them in interviews is because they don't want to be confrontational. Disagree politely and graciously, and there should be no problem. Apologising for disagreeing (without grovelling!) is easy and doesn't seem too submissive:

'I'm sorry, I don't agree. I've always thought that . . .'

> Disagreeing isn't always a complete 'no-no' with interviewers. Better to stand up for yourself and disagree without confrontation than to be caught out in a lie later.

Summary points

♦ Remember the golden rule – people like people like themselves. Matching where possible to establish common ground and rapport is your aim.

♦ Beware of using negative body language and try to make a positive impression on your interviewer by using positive body language.

♦ Eye contact is absolutely critical. But don't overdo it, and make sure you use listening or speaking eye contact as appropriate.

♦ Listening needs to be an active process, so don't just sit there – You need to be seen to be listening!

♦ Mirroring is something that is hard to do properly. Leave well alone unless you are confident in your ability to do it well.

♦ Disagreeing with your interviewer is fine so long as you do it appropriately, and aren't in any way confrontational or aggresive.

Chapter 6

Answering Questions

People get very hung up about being questioned at interview. It's not actually the biggest problem you'll have to tackle in your interview, and let's face it, you should know the answers if you are being asked about yourself!

In this Chapter:

♦ **understanding good questions**
♦ **dealing with bad questions**
♦ **correcting mistakes**
♦ **reinforcing your message.**

Being questioned about your CV, your skills and experience is the real core of an interview. Only by doing this can the interviewer establish whether or not you are a good fit with the requirements of the position for which you are being interviewed.

Everyone attending an interview expects to be questioned. Perhaps that is why answering questions gets blown up out of all proportion in many people's minds, and why they get so worked up about finding good answers to them.

The bulk of questions in any interview will be about you – what you've done, how you think and behave, what you think and feel. There is no reason why anyone should worry about answering this sort of question, as you know yourself (and therefore the answers) better than anybody! But what concerns everyone is how to present those answers in the best possible light – how to make yourself look really good at interview. Understanding questions and answers can help here.

Is this you?

♦ I hate interviews. I just feel like I'm being interrogated, no matter how nice they are.

♦ I know my own life, but I just panic when the questions start – some people word them so awkwardly I can't tell what they really want me to say!

♦ Anyone can answer a simple question – it's getting it just right so I look better than the others that counts.

♦ If the interviewers knew how to ask questions better it would be easier! Half the time I can't answer the question, because it isn't what they actually want to know . . . .

Understanding good questions

The aim of an interviewer is to get you to tell them

what they need to know, in order to make their decision. They need to get you to talk, so they can listen and pick out the information they need. So the aim of any question isn't necessarily to 'catch you out', it's simply to get you to talk to them!

Good questions

There are three main types of 'good questions':

♦ open questions

♦ probing questions

♦ forced choice questions.

Open questions

These are questions with no set answer, which force you to talk freely. For example:

♦ 'Tell me about your time at . . .'

♦ 'Talk me through your last three jobs.'

♦ 'Tell me a little bit more about . . .'

♦ 'What do you think you gained from that?'

Probing questions

These are questions which force you to go into a little more detail. They require less of an answer, but a more specific answer. Probing questions tend to use the words:

♦ 'Who . . . ?'

- 'What . . . ?'

- 'Where . . . ?'

- 'When . . . ?'

- 'How . . . ?'

- 'Why . . . ?'

Forced choice questions

Forced choice questions are designed to put you on the spot. They force you to make a choice of answer. As questions they are actually not as good as the other two types, as they can often be answered with one or two words, or even a 'Yes' or 'No', which doesn't really encourage you to talk. For this reason they are usually followed up with a probing question, such as 'Why?' or 'Could you explain that?' Here are some examples of forced choice questions:

- 'Did you enjoy that type of work or not?'

- 'Do you prefer tasks in stages or whole projects to get on with?'

- 'Are you very organised or more spontaneous?'

- 'Do you get more satisfaction from team work or achieving something alone?'

Good questions are designed to make you talk, so try to give full answers, not just a couple of words. Explain without being asked to – it helps the interviewer.

Dealing with bad questions

Bad questions are questions that close you down, and make it easy for you to say very little. They are also questions that don't actually give the interviewer any useful information about you or your suitability for the job. Good interviewers don't ask bad questions, but here are some of the types of bad questions you may be asked at interview.

Closed questions

Closed questions are poor interview technique because they only require a very short or simple 'Yes' or 'No' answer. They 'close you down' and either prevent you from saying very much, or let weak candidates get away without elaborating their answers. But occasionally an interviewer may use them deliberately, for example when short of time or if you have been giving long answers.Here are some examples:

♦ 'Did you like working there?'

♦ 'How many staff did you have?'

♦ 'Were you there long?'

If you are asked a closed question, deal with it by answering in a reasonable amount of depth anyway – as if the interviewer had asked you to expand your answers.

Leading questions

Leading questions are questions that tell you exactly what answer the interviewer wants you to give. Asking leading questions is bad because it enables weak candidates to get away with doing fairly well at interview – as they can guess what the interviewer wants them to say! It's also bad for strong candidates, as it makes it hard for them to disagree with the interviewer without knowing that this will be unexpected and unwelcome. Here are some examples of leading questions:

♦ 'So you liked it there?'

♦ 'I've always thought X, don't you agree?'

♦ 'I assume you left because . . .'

♦ 'That was a pretty senior role, wasn't it?'

Deal with leading questions by standing up for yourself. Try the 'Yes, but . . .' approach – it could work well for you.

Multiple questions

Multiple questions are where the interviewer asks several questions at once. They are bad questions because they confuse candidates, and make it hard for them to create a good impression by giving the interviewer the information he/she wants. Here are some examples of multiple questions:

♦ 'Did you like working there? They're fairly laid back, aren't they?'

♦ 'What would you choose, why would that particularly be your first choice, and do you foresee any particular problems?'

♦ 'Why did you leave there – I imagine it must have been a wrench – didn't you work there for quite some time?'

Deal with multiple questions by answering all parts of the question if possible. Organise your thoughts by numbering the questions, for example: 'Firstly, I didn't, and secondly, that was because . . .'. It will help you remember to answer all the questions within the question. If you lose track, just ask politely for them to repeat the question: often they will make it easier to understand the second time around.

Hypothetical questions

Hypothetical questions make you use your imagination. That may not sound terribly bad, but it means you aren't being allowed to give the interviewer facts, only conjecture. It can often indicate a weak interviewer, and yet these questions are all too common. Here are some examples:

♦ 'What do you think you would do if . . . ?'

♦ 'How would you handle a customer who . . . ?'

♦ 'If you had been in charge, how would you have handled it?'

♦ 'Why do you think we put that in the advert?'

To stand out from other candidates, deal with hypothetical questions by treating them as if they were asking for facts anyway. 'Well, when I worked at X I had to do that, and I handled it like this . . .'. This will make you stand out from weak candidates who are speaking from guesswork and imagination, not demonstrating experience and skill.

> Interviewers aren't all fantastic and experienced at asking questions – you may need to help them out, by dealing well with bad questions.

Correcting mistakes

It's not strictly speaking answering questions, but at some stage in an interview, you may well find yourself having to correct a mistake. For example, you may be asked a question which isn't accurate: 'Presumably you've worked with . . . before?' Or, you may be in the interview and suddenly it becomes apparent that the interviewer has got something wrong.

Deal with mistakes immediately

When there is an obvious mistake, deal with it immediately. Letting it go out of politeness may seem the safest option – in the short term, it is. After all, it might be just a slip of the tongue, such as referring to the wrong company or something minor like calling you Mark instead of Mike.

On the other hand, it could be a much more significant mistake – the interviewer may have totally got the wrong idea about something. Letting it go can be dangerous because it may come up again. And the longer you let the interviewer go on believing something and saying it without being corrected, the more confusing it is for the interviewer when you eventually correct him/her.

How to interrupt

If an interviewer makes a mistake, the best way to deal with it is to interrupt him/her. Interrupting is usually a negative behaviour, and something that you should avoid, but in this instance, you need to nip things gently in the bud, and correct any apparent mistake immediately. Here are some tips on how to do it:

♦ Interrupt gently. Interrupting is normally regarded as negative behaviour, so make sure you do it politely.

♦ Apologise for interrupting: 'Sorry, but . . .' People often say that apologising makes you look weak and submissive, but it is perfectly all right to apologise (without making a huge issue of it) if you are interrupting someone – in fact under these circumstances, it's appropriate.

♦ Make eye contact. Look at the interviewer when interrupting him/her – it grabs his/her attention.

♦ Raise your hand slightly, palm towards them. This is a 'stopping signal' in body language, and makes it easier for them to stop and listen to you. It shouldn't be a dramatic gesture like a policeman directing traffic, or like a schoolboy asking teacher a question – just a slight movement is all that is necessary.

♦ Point out the interviewer's error politely: 'Sorry, but it was actually XYZ Ltd, not ABC Limited where I did . . .'.

♦ Smile – it never does any harm!

> Nip misconceptions in the bud before they continue. You are building up a picture with the interviewer, and you need to make sure it is a correct one.

Reinforcing your message

Sometimes you may feel you have not said, or been given the chance to say, exactly what you wanted to say. You may want to reinforce your message.

Convincing people by body language

There are certain ways you can convince an interviewer you are telling the truth:

♦ eye contact – meet their gaze steadily and don't look away

♦ hand on heart – touch your heart or chest when making an important point

♦ nod whilst you speak.

Strengthening and emphasising your message

♦ Reinforce your message by repeating it – not too emphatically, just say it then repeat it once.

♦ Reflect back what they say then lead on from there to make your own point. For example: 'I know you've said the job is mainly working on X, so I'd like to make sure you realise just how experienced at this I am.'

Convincing people of the major points you are trying to make can make the difference between an average interview and a performance that will be remembered.

Summary points

♦ **Good questions are easy to answer, so use the time to relax and enjoy yourself! Listen carefully and answer the question.**

♦ **Help the interviewer. Poor questioning technique makes it easy for candidates to give poor answers. Read between the lines and give them the information you think they seek, however badly they phrase the question.**

♦ **Ask for clarification if you need to.**

♦ **When you need to correct an interviewer's mistakes, be polite but factual. Don't just let it go – it may cause problems later.**

♦ **Be honest and truthful, and use body language to impress on the interviewer that you are doing so where necessary.**

Chapter 7

Leave on a Good Note

You'll never make a good first impression on your way out of an interview! But what you can do is blow a good performance by leaving on a low note, or worse, creating a last-minute negative impression.

In this Chapter:

♦ **saying goodbye**
♦ **being remembered**
♦ **final points.**

We have said that the impression people get of you when you first meet can be lasting and very important. Similarly, when you part, you can either reinforce a good impression or ruin all your good work – people do tend to remember the last thing you said or did.

You know the issues about standing up, shaking hands, what to say etc, that we looked at in earlier chapters. Oddly, the relief that you can feel when a stressful interview is over can also affect your behaviour and co-ordination, as your body releases a flood of new hormones and chemicals into your body's bloodstream.

Stay cool and polished until out of sight and earshot of your interviewer – manage your exit in the same way you managed your entrance, and everything will be fine. But you can also use the last few minutes or seconds of your interview to enhance your chances with a good positive sales pitch.

Is this you?

♦ When it's over, I can't wait to get out of there! I can't be bothered with anything but getting away as quickly as possible so I can relax.

♦ I hate that awkward couple of minutes at the end when you're both 'wrapping things up'. I never know what to do.

♦ You can't prepare for the end of an interview – it all depends how well it's gone.

♦ If the first impression counts for so much, why worry about what happens on the way out?

Saying goodbye

The interviewer will usually signal that the interview is at an end.

What to do

♦ Stay seated until the interviewer gets up.

♦ But gather your things together, so there aren't any awkward pauses when you're ready to leave.

♦ Try to avoid grabbing a hasty last mouthful of water or coffee – it looks rushed and rather odd.

What to say

♦ Let the interviewer say 'Goodbye' then respond appropriately.

♦ If he/she doesn't, take the initiative and just say 'Goodbye' politely.

♦ Compliment them (but not excessively!) by saying, for example: 'It was nice to meet you', or 'It's been a pleasure.'

♦ Shake hands. If they don't offer their hand, offer yours first.

♦ Remember what we have said about handshakes. Even if you feel you've done badly, offer a handshake that is confident.

Leaving the room and building

♦ Keep up your best behaviour until you are out of the interviewer's sight and hearing.

♦ Remember: you never know who may be around, so be careful to stay professional until you leave the building – you may be on a security camera!

♦ Don't forget to say 'Goodbye . . . and thank you!' to receptionists.

Interviewers may need help closing the interview – many of them find this the most difficult part, so you may have to take the initiative!

Being remembered

Prepare good questions

At the end of an interview, you will usually be asked whether you have any questions. Prepare some in advance to make sure you always have one or two, as this helps to make interviewers think you are seriously interested in the job.

On the other hand, don't go in with a long list – it's daunting for interviewers and puts them on the spot. Just think of a maximum of, say, three questions. It's fine to write them down, but don't make a shopping list!

Smile and be charming

If you have made any mistakes, or if you have been very serious and professional during the rest of the interview, this is the time when you can now smile and appear a little more relaxed. Often, interviewers who have been nervous will relax at this point too, so this may be a good chance to find out more about the company as the atmosphere starts to relax at last.

You want to leave the impression that you would be a good part of the organisation's team, so you want to appear likeable. If you are now asking questions, be especially friendly. The interviewer has been in charge up to this point, asking all the questions. Suddenly, this can be where you get to put him/her on the spot, so be nice about it as he/she can feel under pressure. You want him/her to feel comfortable with you after you have left.

Questions *not* to ask

♦ 'How did I do?' (or any words to that effect). This shows lack of confidence and you may not have done that badly.

♦ 'Is X a problem?' Don't ever highlight problems on the way out. Better by far to hope they have forgotten X (a bad point) and instead highlight Y (your good point) in some way.

♦ 'If I don't get this job can you keep me in mind for anything else?' (or words to that effect!). This just makes you look desperate for work, and it won't do you any favours.

Raise concerns and deal with them

If you think the interviewer has any unstated concerns, or if he/she has expressed any, try to deal with them. For example, an interviewer might say to you that he/she is not sure whether or not your skillset would fit within the team, but that he/she wants to interview several people to see who would be the best fit with their requirements. At the end of the interview, you could address this issue if you felt it would help create or reinforce a positive impression: 'I remember you mentioned the team fit. Can I just say that the team you described is very similar to the one I'm in at present, and I'm sure I could adapt to any differences quickly.'

Obviously, this is a matter for your personal judgement – the golden rule is to finish on a positive note, and to raise nothing negative at the end of your interview.

> When it is your turn to ask questions, don't try to interview the interviewer – he/she won't like it!

Final points

Putting right things that have gone wrong

If anything went badly, such as you being late, or misunderstanding a question completely, bring it up again and put it right if you can. Obviously, if you can't put it right, don't raise it, or you will end on a negative, but where you can, do so: 'I'm so sorry I misinterpreted what you were saying. I hope you'll be able to see now that actually I've got quite a lot of experience at X.'

Having the last word

If you can prepare a few 'parting shots' that are really positive, commit them to memory so you can use whichever seems most appropriate on the day. For example: 'It's been a pleasure to meet you – I've really enjoyed learning more about what you do.'

What *not* to say

♦ 'I really hope to hear from you.'

♦ 'Please don't forget to let me know about the outcome.'

♦ 'Sorry for being late!' (Don't remind them about bad points at this stage)

♦ 'Good luck with the other interviews!'

♦ 'I hope you find the right person.' (Remember, you should assume *you* are the right person – that's the image you want to cultivate.)

♦ 'Thank you for seeing me.'

> This is your very, very last chance to make a good impression. Never jeopardise it by saying anything negative.

Summary points

♦ **Saying a good goodbye is almost as important as making a good greeting. Plan it carefully in advance.**

- Make sure you are remembered by preparing a couple of short 'closers', using the ones that are most appropriate at the time.

- Always leave on a positive note; never ever leave on a negative note.

Psychometric Tests for Graduates

Gain the confidence you need to excel at graduate-level psychometric and management tests

Andrea Shavick

This book contains 37 genuine graduate-level practice tests from SHL Group plc, the biggest test publisher in the world; 227 questions covering verbal, numerical, abstract and spatial reasoning, mechanical comprehension, fault diagnosis, accuracy and personality; and genuine practice *Brainstorm*, *Scenarios* and *Fastrack* management tests. Research methods are also covered.

ISBN 978-1-84528-262-2

Practice Psychometric Tests

How to familiarise yourself with genuine recruitment tests and get the job you want

Andrea Shavick

Following the success of Andrea Shavick's *Passing Psychometric Tests* and *Psychometric Tests for Graduates* comes this book, crammed full of even more genuine practice psychometric tests from SHL Group plc, the biggest test publisher in the world. They are the tests used by over 95% of the FTSE 100 companies to select their staff, as do the police, the Civil Service, the Armed Forces . . . the list is endless. So if you're looking for a job, you need this book!

ISBN 978-1-84528-020-8

Management Level Psychometric & Assessment Tests

Everything you need to help you land that senior job

Andrea Shavick

Whether you're after a junior management, senior management or even director level position, or simply want to familiarise yourself with the very latest selection and recruitment techniques this book will meet your needs. It includes:

◆ 35 genuine management levels practice psychometric tests and a guide to online testing.

◆ Everything you need to know about personality questionnaires, plus loads of practice material.

◆ A complete guide to what to expect and how to survive an assessment centre visit.

◆ Detailed information on high-level assessment centre exercises commonly used to test candidates.

◆ A guide to researching your chosen organisation.

ISBN 978-1-84528-028-4

How to be Headhunted

The insider's guide to making executive search work for you

John Purkiss & Barbara Edlmair

If you're looking for a senior executive position – or a seat on the board – this book will tell you what you need to know.

◆ Learn about the search industry and the prominent firms within it

- Understand the recruitment process and make it work to your advantage
- Prepare a persuasive covering letter and a 'head-hunter-friendly' CV

Headhunting has long been shrouded in mystique. This book is *the* insider's guide, packed with practical tips to help you approach executive search firms.

ISBN 978-1-84528-048-2

How To Write a Great CV

Prepare a powerful CV that really works
Paul McGee

This book will help you get your foot in the door – and get that interview. You know you can do the job you're going for, but how do you convince the person you are applying to? What you need is a well-designed CV, and that's where this book will help.

Paul McGee provides insights and tips gained from helping thousands of people from all ages and backgrounds to market themselves successfully.

'This book contains useful specimen CVs, covering letters and case studies, together with sample jobs, action plans and interview preparation tips.' *Office Secretary*

ISBN 978-1-84528-892-7

How To Books are available through all good bookshops, or you can order direct from us through Grantham Book Services.

Tel: +44 (0)1476 541080
Fax: +44 (0)1476 541061
Email: orders@gbs.tbs-ltd.co.uk

Or via our website

www.howtobooks.co.uk

To order via any of these methods please quote the title(s) of the book(s) and your credit card number together with its expiry date.

For further information about our books and catalogue, please contact:

How To Books
Spring Hill House
Spring Hill Road
Begbroke
Oxford OX5 1RX

Visit our web site at

www.howtobooks.co.uk

Or you can contact us by email at info@howtobooks.co.uk

THE SCORE

THE SCIENCE OF
THE MALE SEX DRIVE

FAYE FLAM

AVERY

A MEMBER OF PENGUIN GROUP (USA) INC.

NEW YORK

Published by the Penguin Group

Penguin Group (USA) Inc., 375 Hudson Street, New York, New York 10014, USA • Penguin Group (Canada), 90 Eglinton Avenue East, Suite 700, Toronto, Ontario M4P 2Y3, Canada (a division of Pearson Canada Inc.) • Penguin Books Ltd, 80 Strand, London WC2R 0RL, England • Penguin Ireland, 25 St Stephen's Green, Dublin 2, Ireland (a division of Penguin Books Ltd) • Penguin Group (Australia), 250 Camberwell Road, Camberwell, Victoria 3124, Australia (a division of Pearson Australia Group Pty Ltd) • Penguin Books India Pvt Ltd, 11 Community Centre, Panchsheel Park, New Delhi–110 017, India • Penguin Group (NZ), 67 Apollo Drive, Rosedale, North Shore 0632, New Zealand (a division of Pearson New Zealand Ltd) • Penguin Books (South Africa) (Pty) Ltd, 24 Sturdee Avenue, Rosebank, Johannesburg 2196, South Africa

Penguin Books Ltd, Registered Offices: 80 Strand, London WC2R 0RL, England

First trade paperback edition 2009

Most Avery books are available at special quantity discounts for bulk purchase for sales promotions, premiums, fund-raising, and educational needs. Special books or book excerpts also can be created to fit specific needs. For details, write Penguin Group (USA) Inc. Special Markets, 375 Hudson Street, New York, NY 10014.

Library of Congress Cataloging-in-Publication Data

Flam, Faye.
The score : the science of the male sex drive / Faye Flam.
p.   cm.
Includes bibliographical references and index.
ISBN 978-1-58333-349-5
1. Men—Sexual behavior.   2. Men—Health and hygiene.   3. Men—Psychology.   I. Title.
HQ28.F59   2009   2008054335
306.7081—dc22

Printed in the United States of America
1   3   5   7   9   10   8   6   4   2

BOOK DESIGN BY NICOLE LAROCHE

FOR MY PARENTS,
BERNARD AND EVELYN FLAM

CONTENTS

PREFACE

When I was asked to write a sex column for the *Philadelphia Inquirer*, some of my colleagues advised against it. I was already an established science writer, they warned. Why would I want to risk my reputation writing about something potentially sordid—even obscene? Others were sure that I'd be stalked by perverts and would need to walk around the city in disguise.

But I chose to do it anyway. Since there was no rule that I couldn't use science in the column—which was called "Carnal Knowledge"—I started covering everything from the genetics of homosexuality to the chemistry of orgasm to the question of whether our human ancestors had sex with Neanderthals.

I used evolution to explain sex, and I used sex to explain life. I investigated the origin of sex, the first organisms to divide into males and females, and the origins of human sexual morality. I included some evolutionary psychology in the column but tempered it with other branches of psychology, as well as molecular and evolutionary biology, archaeology, anthropology, sociology, genetics, and occasionally botany.

I enlisted the wisdom of theologians to answer questions about the purported maleness of God, the genetics of Jesus, and the prospect of sex in heaven. I called upon linguists to find out whether all cultures swear using a slang term for sexual intercourse.

I often delved into the inflammatory realm of male-female differences, trying to separate the science from the old-style sexist platitudes about male promiscuity on the one hand and politically correct rhetoric about equality on the other.

No one had ever done anything quite like this column, especially for a newspaper as tradition-steeped as the *Inquirer*.

After more than a year of producing a "Carnal Knowledge" column every week, I started thinking I could weave some of the amazing things I'd learned into a book. But with the proliferation of sex books on the market, I knew I needed an unusual angle. When an editor at Avery said I should write about the evolution of the male sex, I agreed to give it a try.

Over the course of my research, I found there were many things of interest to say about males but all of them involved either how males differ from females or how the two sexes relate to each other. So the book is almost as much about women as men. In humans and many other animals, the male sex was shaped largely by the competition for sex and by the preferences of the female sex. Our ancestral women were responsible for shaping men. And men were, to some extent, responsible for the appearance and traits of women. In the following pages I hope to explain how this happened and where it led us.

I owe eternal gratitude to my editor, Trish Wilson, and former executive editor, Amanda Bennett, for having the courage to start an experimental sex column and for handling the onslaught of irate phone calls that followed in my wake. Thanks to Karl Stark, Don Sapatkin, Pete Clarey, and other great talents at the *Inquirer* who polished my columns with their editing and reined me on occasion, and to our current leader at the *Inquirer*, Bill Marimow, for his unwavering support for this project. I'd also like to thank our publisher, Brian Tierney, for embracing risk, having a sense of humor, and fielding many angry and sometimes deranged complaints about my column.

Thanks to all the many scientists in Philadelphia and elsewhere who let me interview them for the column, and to my agent, John Thornton, and my editor at Avery, Jeff Galas, for making it all happen.

I owe a special debt of gratitude to Paul Nussbaum and Anthony Gottlieb for their excellent editorial advice and to Scott Gilbert and Leonard Finegold for making sure I didn't bungle the science. Thanks to my friend Ruth Weisberg for her wit and warmth and homemade chicken soup.

Finally, I should thank my man, Mitch Grieb, for fearlessly accompanying me to Iceland's penis museum, for finding some way to explain to his mother that I was writing a book about sex, and for acting as living proof that men are not pigs.

1. THE MYSTERY

WHAT PICKUP ARTISTS REVEAL
ABOUT THE NATURAL WORLD

I t was the ultimate infiltration into a man's world. I stepped off a train at New York's Penn Station and headed up Eighth Avenue toward a place called the Ripley-Grier Studios. There, I was to witness a "boot camp" for prospective pickup artists. I'd been invited by a publicist for Erik von Markovik, a.k.a. Mystery—a pickup artist, magician, and the main character in Neil Strauss's 2005 bestseller *The Game.*

Von Markovik was not just a pickup artist but a pickup guru with a worldwide network of male admirers and disciples. Some of those disciples were teaching his "method" everywhere from Las Vegas to Sydney. He'd also laid out his technique in his own book, *The Mystery Method: How to Get Beautiful Women into Bed.*

The class, officially called Seduction Boot Camp, was one of several offerings I'd found on a pickup artists' website. The goal, as advertised, is to equip men with a method to get women into bed within seven hours of meeting them. It cost $2,150 a head and included three days of six-hour classroom seminars plus several nights of in-the-field training amid New York's nightclub scene.

The instructor for this one was a twenty-six-year-old U.S. Marine and part-time stand-up comic who went by the moniker Future. In a phone conversation several days earlier, he'd admitted that before he took the course himself in 2004 he had trouble attracting women. "I had this image that New York would be rife with women clamoring to get some veteran ass," he said, but somehow, they weren't.

Being a U.S. Marine and having fought in Iraq didn't help him because he'd drive women away before he'd get the chance to segue his service into the conversation. "My natural personality is rather exuberant," he said, "but I had to moderate my behavior so it didn't look like I was having a verbal seizure." But his transformation wasn't so simple. The method involves many steps and repeated practice. As I thumbed through von Markovik's book, I saw he'd included more acronyms, flowcharts, and diagrams than you'd find in a Space Shuttle flight plan.

It's a very systematic procedure that breaks down into nine steps—three parts of attraction (A1, A2, and A3), three parts of comfort building (C1, C2, and C3), and three parts of sex (S1, S2, and S3). You start the whole thing by approaching a "set," then pick a "target," throw her a "neg," assess her IOIs, use your wingman to help you with a DHV, then, working your way from the final attraction phase, A3, you change location for C1 through C3, always ready to counter her ASD and disarm or escape the AMOG. Who ever said women were the more complicated sex?

I'll explain what all that means later, but in any case, if all goes as planned, you get to S3, which is the goal, the end point, the score. It's become popular wisdom that modern society puts too much emphasis on sex, and yet we may really underestimate its importance in shaping the living world. Not only is the desire for sex etched into the human psyche by eons of evolution, but sex itself guides evolution's course.

Competition for sex pushes the evolution of males and females in different directions. With the popular discussion of human sex differences mired in political controversy, why not move forward by examining ourselves in the bigger context of the natural world? Males, for example, face many common challenges, whether they're penguins or peacocks, Marines with flattops or marine flatworms, or even male wildflowers growing along the side of the road.

At this point it might help to clarify the universal definitions of male and female. Males don't necessarily have to have penises. Penguins and many other birds and fish lack one. They're not always bigger than their female counterparts—many male animals are much smaller. Not all males carry Y chromosomes, either. The natural world employs dozens of different ways to determine who's a girl and who's a boy.

Stripped down to its essentials, the universal defining quality of males is the creation of sperm. And the universal defining quality of sperm is that they're smaller than eggs. Because their sperm are relatively small, males usually make more of them than their female counterparts make eggs. That little asymmetry lies at the root of all sex differences, from the male robin's song, the buck's antlers, and the elephant seal's tonnage to the pickup artist's lines, or at least the desire to learn lines.

The people running the pickup seminars weren't secretive about their teachings. They had no problem inviting me, a female journalist, to listen in. And since they greeted my request to audit their class with such open-mindedness, I tried to extend the same attitude toward them. Who knew what useful insights I might discover?

Seduction Boot Camp was held in a small mirrored dance studio, adjoining other rooms where young dancers were quietly warming up in the hall. The class was an intimate affair, especially since one of the five students who prepaid didn't show up, claiming a concussion. So it came down to me, four male students, and our instructor, Future, sitting in plastic chairs arranged in a circle.

Future looked younger than his twenty-six years —tall but with a layer of baby fat cushioning his cheeks, neck, and middle. He wore a Superman T-shirt, which added to the impression he was just a big kid. He wasn't a bad-looking guy, though there was something odd about his shoes.

After some small talk, our Marine/stand-up comic instructor asked each of the students to answer a few questions: who he was, why he wanted to take boot camp, when (or if) he lost his virginity, and how many women he'd had sex with.

The first student was a thirty-eight-year-old with a faint country twang in his voice that was hard to place—later he revealed he'd lived in Alaska before moving to New York. He'd made plenty of money recently and was taking some time off to find himself, he said. In his real estate business he'd always gotten what he wanted from people, but in love it was a different story. He seemed like a nice country boy until he revealed that after he lost his virginity at eighteen or so, he'd had sex with about twenty prostitutes and a dozen or so other women. "I do want the picket fence," but before he found his fence-mate, he said, "I'd like to have lots of good sex."

The next to tell all was a lanky red-haired young man of twenty-nine who said he'd also lost his virginity around eighteen, slept with a handful of women, and still sought that elusive soul mate and perfect woman. He wanted her to be not just beautiful but a "solid person," he said, not flaky or superficial. The third student, a twenty-nine-year-old stockbroker and casino gambler, said his job had him shuttling between New York and London. He'd been banned from several casinos in Las Vegas for winning too much money. A man like that should have exuded confidence, but instead he slouched, as if hiding, and spoke in a barely audible mumble.

Then there was the oddball of the group—a tall, buff, personal trainer and part-time model who looked like a cross between Tom Cruise and a young John Travolta. He said he was there partly to write a column for a fledgling *Men's Magazine,* but he had also paid for the seminar. He had lost his virginity at sixteen and since then had slept with more than 200 women, he said, many of them glamorous models and actresses.

His revelation was met with a stunned silence. Future finally broke in to ask the obvious question: "Why are you here?"

"I'm a perfectionist," said the model/trainer. "I guess I want to be perfect in everything." And he hated getting stuck in those three-week-long dry spells, he said as everyone in the class winced—Future included. But like all the other guys, he would like to get married someday. He'd turned forty recently, he said. "My parents are hoping I'll settle down."

It took a few seconds for Future and the other regular guys to recover from all this. The taller version of Tom Cruise was an alpha male, the arch enemy of the beta males who made up the usual customers of Mystery Method boot camps. The method's acronym AMOG stands for "alpha male of the group," and according to the method you need to identify and disarm him so he doesn't beat you up. But apparently even the big, buffed-up, handsome guys don't always get everything they want. The alpha male of our little group was scribbling notes as fast as the others while Future attempted to explain the complex system known as the Method.

I'll return to the class soon, but first let's connect what's going on there to the rest of the natural world. At the heart of the Mystery Method is what the guru, von Markovik, calls S and R—survival and replication. I'm pretty sure from reading his book that he meant survival and reproduction, replication implying some sort of asexual cloning. But perhaps to the pickup artists, reproduction sounded too womanly and reminiscent of pregnancy and dirty diapers. Replication sounded more hip, high-tech, and masculine. In von Markovik's estimate, males are wired to excel more in the S part of the equation, females in R. As we'll see later, he had that part backward. In most animals, males put more emphasis on the R part, sometimes to the detriment of their S.

Future, however, felt he'd proved he could handle the S part at Parris Island boot camp, but he needed Mystery Method boot camp to get his R in line. Neither Mystery nor Future had apparently reproduced, or replicated, but at least they had plenty of practice with the first step, for what it's worth. In the end, the goal of the method was sex. What to do if a baby came of it was beyond the scope of their material.

At some point I asked Future why he thought men needed these courses. He attributed it to changes in male roles. No longer can men go out and kill mastodons to feel necessary, he said.

But was this really the reason behind the demand for the Mystery Method? Who's to say such classes wouldn't have gotten takers during the Stone Age? For all we know there was a caveman version of Seduction Boot Camp. Men I've interviewed nearly always assume that their ancestors had it easier—that women only became discerning and picky in recent times.

I suspect that the problems that confront Future and his pickup artists in training go back much further—to about a billion years ago.

2. LET THERE BE SEXES

WHY THE ORIGIN OF THE SEXES
CHANGED EVERYTHING

The most familiar story explaining the origin of the two sexes comes from the Bible. God made Adam first, and afterward decided to create Eve from one of his ribs. All trouble then ensued from this secondary creation of woman. Still, Genesis mixes several slightly different narratives, and woven into it is another, less familiar passage that proposes a more simultaneous origin of the sexes: "male and female He created them" (Genesis 1:27).

That comes a little closer to the current scientific worldview, though the science also tells us that men and women both evolved from other animals, already divided into male and female. So there must have been a first male something and a first female something. What were they and how did they come about?

The scientific creation story is written in the earth's geologic strata and the many bodies buried there. This so-called fossil record is constantly revised as we discover new clues, but the best reading to date suggests life came along first, then sex, and then sexes. And sex showed up late to the party. By trekking around

Australia and Greenland, sampling and dating the world's oldest exposed rocks, geochemists have scraped up chemical traces of bacteria that go back more than three and a half billion years. That means life colonized the planet not long after it cooled from its molten birth. But the first sexual creatures didn't appear until about 600 million years ago. If you condensed the history of life to a calendar year, sex was invented just around Halloween.

To find out how and why living things started having sex, I canvassed the biology community and kept getting directed to Matthew Meselson, a renowned Harvard University geneticist. Back in the late 1950s he helped figure out how DNA replicates itself. In the 1960s he played a major role in understanding how DNA's genetic code gets transcribed onto other biological molecules. In recent years he's become known for his research and activism in disarmament of the world's chemical and biological weapons. But when I called him, he assured me that the question of sex was a deep one and difficult enough to have held his interest throughout his career.

He told me scientists are debating several theories on the evolutionary advantages of sex. They need something to explain why sex got so popular after it was finally invented. But I also wanted to know how it got started and who did it first. That, he said, is not so well understood. "It was probably some sort of accident." In other words, a few ancient microbes bumped into one another, a few of those merged, some of the genetic machinery got rewired, and hundreds of millions of years later we have Match.com, speed dating, and the Mystery Method.

Though random chance does play a role in evolution, the process is powerfully ordered, both by the force of natural selection and the strict laws of chemistry and physics by which biology must abide. Life is opportunistic, and once it stumbles onto something useful, it usually takes full advantage. That's what seems to have happened with sex, since it's now nearly universal among life forms more complex than *E. coli*. And yet, it's not obvious what the big advantage is, said Meselson. Sex has its drawbacks, at least as a form of reproduction. If you can reproduce asexually, you get to pass on *all* your genes rather than throwing away half and replacing them with genes from someone else, he said. You don't have to waste energy finding, picking up, spending money on, or seducing a mate.

One explanation for the relative scarcity of asexual plants and animals is that they suffer from copying errors with each generation, their genes degrading like photocopies of photocopies of photocopies. (A gene is simply a unit of inheritance, written in a chemical code carried by molecules of DNA.) Clone yourself too many times and you lose the most advantageous genetic combinations. Then they're gone forever, he said. "Sex lets you trade genes back and forth, like shuffling cards and handing each player a new deck." To understand how sex can help clean up the gene pool, imagine that you and your partner each carry a harmful spelling error, known as a mutation. When the male partner makes sperm, he divides the sum total of his genes in half, so each child has a fifty-fifty chance of being produced from a sperm that held his bad mutation. The same thing goes for the eggs—only half of them will carry a single bad mutation.

Now, say the two of you have a whole mess of children. Some may get your mutation but not your partner's and some may get only the partner's, but there's a one-in-four chance that a child will come from a mutation-free sperm and a mutation-free egg. On the downside, there's also a one-in-four chance that a child will get both your bad mutation and your partner's.

If instead of having sex you reproduced by cloning yourself, as bacteria do, your offspring would automatically get stuck with all of your genetic mistakes, and would probably accumulate more. Sex offers the hope of a clean slate—an offspring to pass on just the healthy genes without the garbled ones.

Other scientists have proposed an idea called the Red Queen theory, named after the character in Lewis Carroll's *Through the Looking Glass* who said: "Now, here, you see, it takes all the running you can do, to keep in the same place. If you want to get somewhere else, you must run at least twice as fast as that!" For many living things, you have to keep changing and evolving to stay ahead of parasites, which are forever evolving better ways to infest us. And the best way to stay ahead is to mix up your genes.

Sex might also help creatures defend against other natural hazards beyond just parasites, said Swarthmore College developmental biologist Scott Gilbert. Some species of algae employ sex only when they suffer extreme heat that could potentially wipe them out. Sex allows them the quick genetic reshuffling they need to breed more resilient offspring.

The fossil record does show that once that fateful accident known as sex occurred, everything changed. The seas filled with jellyfish, sponges, sea worms, and other relatively complex life. It seems the invention of sex ushered in a level of complexity that wasn't possible before.

THE PARASITIC SEX?

The invention of mating is just part of the story. It turns out you don't need males to have sex. To understand how sex without sexes could possibly work, I called on Laurence Hurst, a biologist from the University of Bath, in England, who studies the evolution of that male/female divide. Remember that to get males and females you just need to make sperm and eggs, the sperm being defined as the smaller sex cells. The males are then defined as the makers of the sperm.

Hurst told me the scientific term for sex without males or females is "isogamy." It means reproduction not with eggs and sperm but with sex cells of roughly the same size. Many relatively simple organisms still practice isogamy—certain types of algae, fungi, and pond-swimming microbes. Because these organisms trace back so far in the history of life, Hurst said, it appears that isogamy was the ancestral form of sex. So was it really Adam and Steve rather than Adam and Eve? Biologists say the first sexual beings were hovering between maleness and femaleness—so we might better think of them as Pat and Chris. But something broke that perfect symmetry, and it stayed broken in the branches of life that led to plants and animals.

Some biologists say the first sperm and eggs took shape from random fluctuations. Since nothing is perfectly uniform, some sex cells will naturally come out ever so much smaller or larger than the rest. Under certain circumstances, those tiny size differences can get magnified. It's a little like the process that shaped the cosmos, as minuscule fluctuations in the primordial mists got amplified over time into vast strings of galaxies. But in the case of the cosmos, the driving force was gravity, while for life it was natural selection.

Somehow natural selection drove the small sex cells to keep shrinking until they qualified as the first sperm, thus qualifying their producers as the first males. David Hosken, a biologist from

Exeter University in England said the reigning theory explaining this was laid out in the 1970s by three scientists —Parker, Baker, and Smith. Their idea: as soon as some of the sex cells started coming out a little smaller than the rest, the creatures making them could send out more of them. Smaller was cheaper. So eventually you had proto-males making slightly smaller sex cells—proto-sperm—and by doing this they got to pass down a few more copies of their genes than everyone else. And included among those were genes associated with cheapness, which proliferated.

But eventually the proto-males ran into a problem. Once their sex cells shrank past a certain point, they could no longer procreate with each other. Two proto-sperm just didn't have enough substance to start a new life. Suddenly there was a new premium on being big. And for those making large sex cells—proto-females—the bigger you could make them, the better. Only relatively large proto-eggs could make up for the increasing cheapness of the proto-sperm and still successfully reproduce. So the smaller the sperm got, the bigger the eggs had to get. And the bigger the eggs got, the smaller the sperm could get.

Biologists call this process disruptive selection because it pulls different members of a species in different directions. The males compete in a sheer numbers game—whoever makes the most sperm wins. The females compete to create the most self-sufficiently fertile eggs—ones that can grow into viable babies using even the tiniest sperm. The losers are those in the middle, since they can't win either way.

The theory is backed up by computer models simulating the origin of separate sexes in hypothetical living things, as well as by studies of existing organisms. The latter studies bank on the fact that only relatively complex organisms should divide up into males and females, said Hurst. In the case of very simple algae for example, everyone can afford to make tiny sex cells and get away with it. That results in lots of very tiny fertilized eggs, which is fine for them since they don't have to grow into anything too involved. As organisms become more complex, they need a bigger, more substantial fertilized egg to get development started. And that means someone has to provide a relatively big sex cell. That someone is, by definition, the female.

To test that connection between complexity and sexes, Hurst and others look at organisms just on the cusp, barely complex enough to need males and females. One good example is a type of green algae called volvocales, or, more popularly, volvox. It looks like pond scum to us but only because of our limited vision. Under the microscope it resolves into beautiful clusters of emerald spheres. Some species of volvox array more spheres than others, meaning they are more complex and need to start from more substantial beginnings. If the biologists' understanding of the origin of males and females holds up, those volvox species with more spheres should split into separate sexes, while the ones with fewer spheres would get away without it. And that's indeed what the scientists see.

It looks as though once you get past a certain level of complexity, some members have to put up with being female, burdened with the task of producing big, nurturing sex cells. Others took advantage of those nurturing cells to deposit their own cheaply packaged genes. Those would be the males. Looked at this way, males seem to get the better deal, saddling females with most of the burden of reproduction. Hosken said that's just the way it came out. "Males are essentially parasitic on females. . . . What you have here is the primordial sexual conflict." Yet there's a more positive view of the first males, too.

THE CLEANER SEX?

Hurst said there's more to the male role than parasitic opportunism. Males often help the entire species by stepping up to do some critical housekeeping. This cleanliness factor was something Hurst found while exploring a seemingly silly question—why we have *only* two sexes. Most life forms limit themselves to two, though there's no law saying they have to.

It's a deceptively difficult question, he said. "Imagine we're going down to a nightclub and there are three sexes. Then we'd have a sixty-six-percent chance of meeting someone we'd be successful with." Increase that to four or perhaps five sexes and your odds of getting lucky go up even more, since an even greater fraction of the population now represents an "opposite" sex. Even better might be a system with no sexes at all. That way you could mate with anyone. There would be no opposite sex to have to learn to understand. "Two," he said, "is the worst system possible."

A few organisms are blessed with extra sexes, or, more technically, mating types. Pond-swimming paramecia divide themselves into one hundred "sexes," and scientists have caught individuals mating with any of the ninety-nine other ones. Mushrooms take it to extremes, with about 30,000 sexes. It's a system that appears to have evolved because it prevents mushrooms from mating with themselves—something that can harm an organism by compounding genetic defects, just like any other form of incest.

Most living things get only two sexes, even when their sex cells are the same size. When Hurst and other scientists spy on these so-called isogamous organisms, including several species of algae, they find that many naturally divide themselves into two different types. That is, an individual algae cluster only combines its sex cells with those coming from the opposite "sex," or "mating type." They don't qualify as male or female because they don't make sperm or eggs, which are distinguished by size. These organisms make all sex cells the same size, so scientists call these two types, pretty arbitrarily, plus and minus.

Having just two, of course, limits your sexual opportunities to just half the population, said Hurst, but in the 1990s he came up with a theory explaining why most life forms get stuck with this system anyway. He was then working along with the famous Oxford University biologist William Hamilton, who died in 2000. This new theory had to do with keeping control of parasites and preventing your cellular machinery from running amok.

The biggest potential troublemakers are the mitochondria—tiny internal working parts of the cell—or, in the jargon, "organelles." Our mitochondria are essential to our survival, helping convert food to energy. In the 1960s, biologist Lynn Margulis proposed that these weren't just miniature organs. They came equipped with their own genetic codes written in their own DNA, and they packaged that DNA together with some protein-making machinery in their own membranes—like a cell within a cell. To Margulis, they looked suspiciously like bacteria. So she proposed that's where mitochondria originally came from. Formerly free-living bacteria, they invaded our cells some 600 million years ago—around the same time sex was invented—and began to live with us in a mutual codependence known as symbiosis. Her scientific peers dismissed the idea as crazy, but now, decades later, it's become universally accepted.

And while mitochondria seem to be working for us, they have no binding contract to continue to do so, said Hurst. Because mitochondria carry their own DNA, they have their own evolutionary agendas. They multiply their numbers of their own accord, without waiting for our cells to divide. During those divisions they will occasionally mutate and can, in theory, spawn a new strain of mitochondria that's very good at replicating itself but not very good at doing its job of helping us make energy. These new unfriendly mitochondria could start to spread through the population at our expense, like an infection.

This is not just a theoretical disaster scenario, said Hurst. It's really happened in yeasts, which get overrun with bad mitochondria, becoming what are called "petite" mutants.

With that possibility looming for all mitochondria-carrying organisms, a new pressure arose to develop protection against such an invasion from within. At one point, Hurst said, some organisms acquired a very helpful mutation—one that enabled its owners to kill all mitochondria from their sex partners. If these early "killers" carried well-behaved, healthy mitochondria, they could ensure the continued health of their family lines by destroying any new and potentially faulty or unfriendly ones. Killers would start to proliferate, but they couldn't mate with other killers or they would produce offspring with no mitochondria and hence no power. To prevent a massive mitochondria slaughter, some organisms had to remain nonkillers. The killers and nonkillers then started to develop strategies to avoid mating with their own types. Heterosexuality was thus born.

It's not clear exactly how this translated into our system of male and female. In us humans, sperm shed most of their mitochondria as they form, stripping down to little more than a package of DNA with a tail. The few mitochondria that remain in the sperm get killed by the egg. Hurst said the most likely possibility is that females evolved from killers and males from nonkillers. If your mate is just going to kill your mitochondria anyway, you don't suffer any big disadvantage if you get rid of them yourself. If you can do this by making your sex cells very small and squeezing most of the mitochondria out, you also benefit by getting rid of viruses and bacteria. So the first male wasn't just cheap—he was hygienic. It's not that the males-as-parasites idea is wrong, said Hurst. It's just that males evolved for other reasons as well.

Eggs can transmit a host of dangerous hangers-on, said Hurst, including viruses, bacteria, mycoplasmas, protozoans, fungi, and spirochetes. He said we live in a delicate balance with our germs—it's in their evolutionary best interest not to kill us if we're providing room and board. But that balance gets thrown off when an organism accumulates different strains of invaders. Males help keep the whole thing under control by squeezing the invaders out of their sperm.

In the end, said Hurst, this system of mitochondria and germ control works best with just two sexes. In theory, it could include more, if you used some kind of complicated circular hierarchy—say, sex number 1 kills mitochondria from sex number 2, and sex 2 kills those from sex 3, and sex 3 kills those from sex 1. But in nature, what you see is usually just two sexes. The occasional exceptions to that rule find ways to exchange genetic material without letting much else pass between them. Such organisms need the equivalent of a mitochondria-catching condom.

If you're a pond-swimmer called a ciliate paramecium, for

example, you can have sex with about ninety-nine of the total one hundred sexes, but to do so you divide your chromosomes in half, sidle up to a mate (which can be anyone), and trade half of your genes for half of its. That way you don't exchange any mitochondria. But both of you come away from the encounter with a new genetic identity. By having sex you become identical twins. "You'd be half me and I'd be half you," said Hurst. You can each then divide in two and become identical quadruplets. In a way, the original parents are lost, but on the bright side, no one has to die.

If you're a horny mushroom looking to hook up with a member of one of the 29,999-odd other sexes, you also have to engage in an unusual sort of sex. All the action happens underground, said Hurst. It's there that the mushrooms really live, sending out little fibers called mycelia that grow outwards in search of sex. When two of these meet, they trade cell nuclei—packages of chromosomes that they shuttle up to the fleshy, and often tasty, part of the mushroom called the fruiting body. The transfer of the genes is like passing security at the Pentagon's inner sanctum. Only those with the right "clearance" can get in while everyone else is blocked. With such a hassle involved in extra sexes, it makes some sense limiting them to two.

Even with males apparently doing a little bit of the cellular housekeeping, our system of two sexes still seems to leave females stuck with most of the burden of baby-making, since we're the ones who have to show up with a sex cell substantial enough to start a new life. But there's a catch to being male. Evolution tends to find ways to even out the burden of reproduction. The males often have to work harder just to get sex in the first place.

3. COMPETING FOR FEMALES

HOW THE QUEST FOR SEX
MADE MEN DIFFERENT FROM WOMEN

Men often say they have to work harder than women to get sex. In a characteristically provocative essay titled "Why Women Aren't Funny," for example, Christopher Hitchens writes, "The chief task in life that a man has to perform is that of impressing the opposite sex. . . . Women have no corresponding need to appeal to men in this way. They already appeal to men. . . ."

Sure, we already appeal once we've dieted, exercised, toned, bikini-waxed, conditioned, moisturized, blow-dried, and plucked our eyebrows. Admittedly, women wouldn't pay over two thousand dollars for a seminar in how to pick up men.

Still, whether or not you agree with his premise that women aren't funny, Hitchens does touch on an interesting scientific question: Is there any reason males have to try harder? To get a scientific answer, I asked Richard Bribiescas, a Yale anthropologist who has taken a special interest in the human male. (His book *Men:*

Evolutionary and Life History was published in 2006.) "The tendency to compete over females is not just universal across cultures but pretty universal across all mammalian species," he told me.

Why would males compete for females and not the other way around? It all depends on an elaborate system of checks and balances. If you put in less work in the parenting department, you often get forced into more work in the seduction/courting arena. In humans and other mammals, for example, females are stuck gestating and nursing babies, while males just have to ejaculate. That allows males, in theory, to produce many more offspring than would be physically possible for a female. The price for that is more competition.

In his book *Sex Wars,* Cambridge University biologist Michael Majerus lays out various reproductive records for female and male animals: in red deer, it's 14 for does to 24 for bucks. For elephant seals, it's 8 for cows and 100 for bulls. For the two-spotted ladybird, it's 2,341 for females and 42,415 for males. When he gets to human beings, he cites the *Guinness World Records* in reporting that the female baby-making record is 69 and for males it's 888. Both figures strain credulity, but not the fact that the male record is more than ten times the female one.

If you have equal numbers of males and females among such species, then some males will do much better than others. For every one that sires dozens or hundreds or thousands of offspring, other males sire few offspring or get left out of the game completely. In order to pass down your genes you have to be bigger, stronger, smarter, better connected, prettier, more tuneful, sneakier, or perhaps funnier than the competition, depending on the particulars of your species.

In his article Hitchens cites little more in the way of evidence than his own experience of being funny and a Stanford University School of Medicine study showing men and women respond differently to cartoons. There are other, more universally popular, ways for men to get ahead, said anthropologist Bribiescas. Cross-cultural studies show men are more driven than women to engage in what he calls "coalescing resources," and those resources could come in the form of land, cattle, yachts, or hedge funds.

The record of 888 children is attributed to an emperor of Morocco known as Moulay Ismail the Bloodthirsty. He doesn't sound like a funny guy, but he probably did coalesce lots of resources. And while his seventeenth-century exploits must rely on estimate or legend, modern DNA work has led some scientists to speculate that super-breeder Genghis Khan disseminated his signature Y chromosome across much of the former Mongolian empire. Scientists disagree over whether this was the doing of the warrior himself or included his brothers and cousins. But either way, he probably didn't achieve this by making them laugh.

While in a few species males seem to avoid all this competition, there's usually a hidden cost somewhere. Some put in extra work later, in the parenting department, and we'll meet a few good fathers later on. In very fatherly animals, males may even be sought out for sex. Harder to explain are the few species in which the males appear to be slackers in both the competitive and sexual arenas.

Take sea urchins, for example. These starfish cousins come in many species, and across the board males aren't any prettier than the females. They aren't any bigger, and they don't do any special courtship behaviors. And sea urchins are not, as far as anyone can tell, funny.

How do they get away with it? I tracked down one of the country's top experts on sea urchins, Florida State University biologist Don Levitan. He told me Charles Darwin himself puzzled over sea urchins because he couldn't see any apparent male/female differences. It's nearly impossible to tell the boy sea urchins from the girl ones. The key to the puzzle is in the way the sea urchins have sex, Levitan said. Biologists have a pretty broad definition of sex, so they consider sea urchins to be sexual creatures even though all they do is cast their sperm and eggs out into the water—a system known as broadcast spawning. That means males can delegate the burden of finding and competing for mates to their sperm, said Levitan. In tide pools crowded with other sea urchins, the males make short-lived but fast sperm that compete by sprinting. But the rarer, and thus more spread out, sea urchins make sperm that have to live a long time and swim vast distances to find eggs of their own species.

Broadcast spawning is probably an ancestral form of sex, said Levitan. Many other sea creatures, including a number of fish, do it this way. And plant sex involves a variation on the broadcast-spawning theme. Some plants are considered bisexual because they bloom with flowers that have both male and female parts. But other plants grow up as either males or females. These straight, hetero plants include marijuana and a weedy shrub called the spice bush. And in those, the male plants get their sperm out by packaging them in aerodynamic vehicles known as pollen grains.

The downside is that the pollen has to work hard. Botanists will tell you that just because female plants are rooted in the ground doesn't make them easy. The hard part is only beginning once that pollen lands on the sex parts of a female plant. It then has to bore its way down to male plant nirvana—the flower's ovary. Along the way, the pollen encounter a series of obstacles set up by the female.

Female plants administer what looks suspiciously like something the pickup artists call the shit test—a series of challenges intended to weed out unworthy suitors. The female flowers attack the pollen with enzymes or salts that blow up all but the toughest of grains. And even then, a male plant could lose to the competition. And just as guys approaching an attractive woman at a bar have to contend with lots of male rivals, so the poor pollen grain still has to race to the ovary against pollen from a bunch of other male plants.

The pressure to compete for females applies whether you're a male human trying to get lucky or a male shrub, says Richard Niesenbaum, a botanist at Muhlenberg College in Pennsylvania. "The goal of male function is to get your sperm out there." He sees this as a common motif throughout the living world: males compete and females put them through the wringer.

At some point, "out there" required a little more precision. In the animal kingdom, there came a point where males and females started pairing up—swimming together as they released sperm and eggs. Others started going to still further extremes to control whose genes would get into their progeny. Copulation, says Levitan, probably evolved independently many times—in vertebrates, in different lines of insects, in squids and their kin. So no one really gets full credit for inventing it. Some scientists make the case that human sperm retain some of their primordial ability to compete with sperm from other men, either by speed, teamwork, or even killing rival sperm. But a member of a copulating species can only delegate so much work to his sperm. The little guys won't get to the playing field unless a man gets off the couch and advocates for them one way or another.

LIVE FAST, DIE YOUNG

Whether men are funnier than women is a matter of debate, but it's harder to deny that men take more risks with their lives than women and therefore tend to die earlier. This tendency set off a skirmish in the war between the sexes in early 2007 when a *New York Times* article proclaimed that slightly more than half of American women were not living with spouses. The same could not be said for men. The *Times* analysis determined that 53 percent of American men were married, compared to 49 percent of American women.

Thousands of people responded, through the *Times* website and on blogs, with comments admonishing today's women for being "selfish," or celebrating us for being "independent." Accusations of man-hating flew. But this imbalance has everything to do with men and not women: it's simply that there are more women in the population.

The census data show that even though a few more boys are born every year than girls, males die at a higher rate in childhood, adolescence, young adulthood, and middle age. In the ninety-plus category, women outnumber men more than three to one. Instead of being worried about the dying institution of marriage, or women's dying interest in wedlock, we should first show some concern for those dying men. One researcher who shares my concern is Daniel Kruger, a social scientist at the University of Michigan. In a recent study, he found that many thousands of American males die prematurely every year. Some were shot, some stabbed, some killed in car crashes. Some had heart attacks, some strokes, some drank themselves to death. "Men tend to die at higher rates than women across the whole life course from each of these major causes with the exception of cancer in middle adulthood," he said.

Kruger also looked at mortality data for eleven other countries as well as among the Ache Indians of South America. Across the board he found many more men than women die before age fifty from accidents or illness. He and other scientists attribute this trend to evolution. It holds not just across cultures but across other animal species as well.

This does not mean men are consciously trying to impress women by shooting at each other or driving too fast. But the tendency to take risks could have evolved in men anyway if women preferred to mate with daredevils and procreated with them before they self-destructed. Risk-taking behavior could then grow and flourish like the elaborate tail of a peacock, which is a dangerous possession in a world of predators. Kruger doesn't think risk taking by itself made women swoon, but it gave men a shot at status, which did. One way men achieved status through the eons was by accomplishing daring, attention-getting feats, he said. So the bravest or most reckless of our male ancestors may have died relatively young but still left behind more offspring than their competitors.

Kruger said testosterone is also to blame. Though both sexes make it, males in most species make significantly more. In birds it brings out the bright colors and songs of the males. In human beings it brings out muscularity, but it also appears to depress men's immune systems and can influence fat metabolism in a way that makes fast food more life-threatening for men. So if we want more potential husbands, especially for older women, then we should encourage men to lay off the Big Macs, drive more carefully, and stay away from guns. Talking to Kruger was sobering.

It made me think differently about the health of my own man and what I might have to do to increase my odds of keeping him around for a few more decades. There's much we can all do for men, including helping them feel wanted without their having to do anything life threatening. Perhaps women always knew this instinctively, which is why we tend to flatter our men and laugh at all their jokes, letting them think they're funnier than women.

4. SEX DRIVE

WHY SOME MALES WILL RISK
LIFE AND LIMB FOR SEX

How far would you go to have sex with your favorite movie star? Would you walk over hot coals to do it with Angelina Jolie? Jump from a plane to get a shot at George Clooney? As I learned from Seduction Boot Camp, men are willing to invest shocking amounts of money, time, and energy in the quest to "get beautiful women into bed," as pickup guru von Markovik so bluntly puts it in the subtitle of his book.

I'll return to the pickup artists shortly and explain just what they're willing to invest in sex. But first let's look at some even more sex-obsessed creatures, willing to risk life and limb for the chance to mate. The most famous examplar of kamikaze sex, the male praying mantis, braves the monster appetite of a much larger female, known to make an appetizer of male heads, and apparently the bodies, too.

"If you put a pair together and come back later, you'll just find the wings of the male and no other evidence he was ever there," said William Brown, an evolutionary biologist at the State University of New York, quoted in a recent *New York Times* article. The article goes on to say that female Chinese mantises make male heads their staple food, composing 63 percent of their diet. Recent research suggests that males try pretty hard not to get eaten. Some try to choose females that just ate something else, for example, though that strategy doesn't always work.

The male mantises are not alone in their plight, as I learned after researching the mysterious deep-sea dweller known as the giant squid. You don't want to mess with a giant squid, even if you yourself are a giant squid. When scientists from Japan released the first-ever video of this elusive creature in 2005, they opened but the smallest glimpse into its mysterious life. Until now, all we knew of the giant squid we learned from dead bodies washed ashore or caught by trawlers.

Steve O'Shea, a giant-squid expert from New Zealand, said males grow to about thirty feet from the top of the mantle to the tips of the tentacles. Females grow up to forty feet. They live in near total darkness several miles below the surface, where they probably spend most of their time eating, fighting off hungry sperm whales, and having sex.

Their sex lives don't look like fun for either party, their embraces ending with maiming and sometimes death. Yet some irresistible force draws them together to procreate. The male faces the greater risk, since the female is usually bigger and there's almost no way for him to mate with her without making her mad.

The male uses his penis like a hypodermic needle, piercing the skin on the female's arms, O'Shea explained, since the female has no vagina. Then, with hydraulic force, the male injects her with four-inch-long tadpole-shaped "spermatophores." They look like giant sperm, but really serve as sperm vehicles. Thousands of actual sperm wriggle inside each one's head.

The penis is about five feet long when flaccid. "I've never seen one erect, and I hope I never will," joked O'Shea, who has been trying to capture a live giant squid for more than a decade. The end of the penis has a cartilaginous lance, he said, the better for stabbing. He paused. Talking about this too much, he observed, can get you labeled as some kind of pervert.

And yet, how can we understand these creatures without looking at their reproductive cycles? Their sex lives make them interesting—perhaps enough to get human beings to care about them. That is critical, O'Shea said, because we don't know how many giant squid are out there, or whether they stand a chance against the voracious deep-sea trawlers pulling up every living thing in their paths—much of it just cast away afterward. As of my 2005 interview with O'Shea, such trawlers had killed at least 121 giant squid, but he and other marine biologists suspect many more deaths go unreported.

The dead ones have revealed what amazing creatures they are—far more bizarre than any space alien dreamed up by science fiction. Scientists have seen the bayonet penises and the sperm-infested arms. They've come across dead squid with eggs, or egg masses, which the female apparently secretes from under her mantle.

The scientists don't know exactly how this process leads to little giant squid. At some point, the female has sperm under her skin and eggs outside her body. The leading theory, O'Shea said, is that she cradles the eggs, bound by a kind of jelly, in her arms. A chemical prompts the spermatophores to burst through her skin, "like parasitic worms."

Worms with heads, that is, and when they slither out of her body, the heads explode, discharging the sperm to go wriggle into the eggs. Is it possible, I asked, that squid don't feel pain the same way we do, and so in some twisted way it could be good for her? He said he doubted that. "It probably hurts like buggery."

Other species of squid employ yet more brutal methods of insemination. One grabs the female with skin-ripping hooks. Another gives her one hard stab in the back. There's just no nice way to inseminate a female in such cases, which creates a problem for the males. Sometimes a female will bite off the male's penis or arms with her deadly beak. It may be that one or both sexes don't survive the encounter. If human males faced these sorts of hazards, it would seem perfectly understandable that they'd gather in pickup classes and related support seminars, there to boost one another's courage to approach the opposite sex.

Which brings us back to the twenty-six-year-old ex-Marine/ comic, Future, and his Seduction Boot Camp. When we left them, they'd just given their introductions and revealed how many women they'd bedded. After that, it was time for Future to launch into the method itself and all the work it entailed. As I touched on briefly back in chapter 1, the method breaks mating down to nine stages: A1, A2, A3, C1, C2, C3, S1, S2, and S3. The men taking the class with me seemed to stumble most often, they said, back in the A's.

Sometimes it was fear that held them back, and sometimes it was plain old cluelessness. Future said that before he discovered the method, his seductions often floundered in the A1 stage because he didn't understand women. In those less polished days he used to walk up to an object of his desire and announce, "You're the most beautiful woman here." He once even followed a woman onto the dance floor to repeat the line before she snapped, "I heard you the first time," as she danced away. Now Future says he understands why that approach was unlikely to get him a second look, let alone sex. The key to all three stages of A is to appear not to be working too hard, Future explained. You have to telegraph the notion that everyone wants you. It's all part of a tactic called DHV, or "demonstration of higher value" in pickup parlance. That means you can't appear needy or desperate. If you're making women think about how they're going to get rid of you, you've lost.

So, to start with, you introduce a "false time constraint," Future told his students. When you approach a group of women, or even a mixed group at a bar, club, or party, he said, you tell them you can only stay a moment because you have to get back to your friends, or catch a train, or something on that order. That way, they won't be thinking about how long they're going to be stuck with you or how they can get you to stop pestering them. It makes you seem in control, and in demand. Then you offer up some kind of conversation topic—say, a story about a friend's bachelor party, or an ex-girlfriend's jealous streak. You ask if they've seen the catfight outside. But instead of planting yourself in front of your target (the woman you want), you address other members of the group so she doesn't think you're chasing her. At that point Future demonstrated the correct body language. You skim by, approaching at an oblique angle, looking sideways over your shoulder. When the target looks at you or says something, you move away, and then, as if on a whim, you return.

He demonstrated this with a little role-playing, pretending he and I were a couple, and later that we were a pair of women in a club and then making the students attempt to pick up on us. Next, he switched roles, so he was playing the pickup artist, to show the students better ways to do it. As a woman, I tried to imagine what I'd do if these guys approached me out at some social venue.

Future's little tricks did, I had to admit, seem amusing. Pickup artists must continually gauge their reactions, seeking IOI, or "indicators of interest" from the opposite sex.

During the A stages it's also important, he said, to convince women that you're popular with other women. That means, if possible, making female friends and bringing them with you, or making some new friends at the club and walking around with them on your arm. They should be good-looking if possible. A more detailed version of this tactic is called pawning. The idea is that when you enter a club or party, you start by picking up a couple of sevens (rated on that odious one-to-ten looks scale). Then you walk up to that ten you had your eye on, with a seven on each arm. That forces a little false competition. In his book, Mystery explains the value of this. "Women will find a man more attractive if he has already been preselected by other women."

I'LL HAVE WHAT SHE'S HAVING

While I didn't find any scientists who'd studied the Mystery Method specifically, some evolutionary psychologists had heard of it and taken an interest, and a few had experimented with some of the broader principles involved, such as being seen with a woman to get another woman. In some animals, females are known to engage in something called "mate copying." Some female birds, in particular, are hardwired to mate only with males that other females have already chosen. This is often no problem for the females since males of many species are happy to accommodate all their groupies. The role models they copy don't even have to be real, as biologist Lee Dugatkin at the University of Louisville discovered a few years ago. He placed a whole flock of stuffed decoy female birds next to certain male birds while leaving the other males to fend for themselves. Copycats that they were, the females ignored the lone males, and instead joined the decoys to mate with one who appeared, at least, to be the life of the party.

Once a pickup artist's first mission is accomplished and he's attracted a woman's attention, there's a whole new challenge. A guy can still flame out pretty easily in the second stage of attraction—A2. It's critical that at this stage you throw in what's called a "neg," which is a negative comment, though it's not an insult, as Future noted. It's a little like big-brotherly teasing, designed to suggest you're not trying to pick up the person you're in fact trying to pick up.

So a neg might be something like, "Those are nice shoes. I saw another girl wearing the same ones earlier." Or you'd turn to her friends and say, "Is she always like this?" or "Where's her off button?" Or you can ask a question to several women, and if the hot babe you've targeted answers, you say, "I didn't ask you." At that stage you can further amp up your magnetism by starting to walk away and looking back over your shoulder. But Future was careful to warn his students that this is a delicate art. "If you neg too hard," he said, "people think you're an asshole."

Playing hard-to-get comes back into the method again in the S phase, which is, of course, sex. First the method advises that you go through the three C stages, for comfort building, which boils down to taking the woman on a couple of dates. Though the method is billed as a technique for getting women into bed after just seven hours, those hours aren't necessarily continuous. Future advises that they should be spread out over several days for best results. Then there's S1, foreplay, which is recommended. S2 has to do with overcoming what these guys call "last-minute resistance." It happens when a woman suddenly changes her mind about a man after she's already in bed with him or close to it, due to jitters, bad breath, sobering up, general revulsion, or fear of coming across as too easy. Future and his colleagues label this ASD, for anti-slut defense. Their solution is to back off. Leave the bed if possible and go work on your computer. Make it easy for her to escape and—they claim—she will lose her resistance and try to lure or cajole you back into bed or even attack you on the office chair. And then, if you're lucky and you do everything right, you get to S3, which is intercourse.

The students jotted down notes as Future explained this, some interjecting questions along the way to make sure they understood whether you should only neg in A2 or also in A3, and whether the first date extended to C3—or was that just C2. It was all very technical. The Tom Cruise look-alike who'd slept with more than 200 women stretched out one of his long legs and rested his foot up on a chair. He seemed to know most of this already. He was stuck in a different rut. He'd already had more S3 than a man deserves in a lifetime. And yet in the grand scheme of life he didn't feel he'd really won.

THE POWER OF PICKINESS

Mystery sums up the pickiness issue this way: "If you take any girl you can get, you must be a loser. But if you are picky, you must be a winner, and her emotional circuitry is designed to respond to winners automatically."

This, too, it turns out, has been studied scientifically. Paul Eastwick of Northwestern University wanted to know whether those who played hard-to-get and appeared very selective did better in the love/dating/sex department than those who came off as undiscerning or desperate. To approach this question, he studied a type of singles event known as speed dating. At these, men and women rotate through a series of three- or four-minute "dates," or chats, after which they all write down which of their possible suitors they'd like to see again. While many commercial outfits offer speed dating, Eastwick and his colleagues staged their own events, enlisting volunteers from among Northwestern's undergraduate population. After they rotated through the series of short interviews, the students were asked to rate how much they'd like to date each of their prospective matches on a scale from one to nine. They were also asked to guess how picky their opposite-sex counterparts had been. The results: the students of both sexes were surprisingly good at surmising who said yes to nearly everyone and who said yes to just one or two people. And there was a definite correlation between how picky you were, how picky people thought you were, and how many people wanted you.

Of course, being attractive can make you picky and also make you desirable. That could be the common element behind the correlation, but Eastwick says he was able to correct for attractiveness. So if you're just as handsome as the next guy but you're *perceived* as less discriminating, in theory you won't come off as well. Eastwick said his results don't reveal how you're supposed to achieve this perception of pickiness, but he thought the Mystery Method could help.

Other scientists have indirectly approached the Mystery Method's mystique by studying the brain. In an essay titled "The Pleasure (and Pain) of Maybe," Stanford University neuroscientist

Robert Sapolsky suggests that introducing an element of uncertainty may send a burst of dopamine through your target's brain. The dopamine circuit, he said, is associated with pleasure and is activated when people use cocaine or indulge in various other sins and addictions. He said he got interested in the "power of maybe" after watching two baboons in the Serengeti, in East Africa. There was a lovelorn male named Jonathan who never stopped chasing an aloof female named Rebecca. The more Rebecca spurned his advances, the more ardently Jonathan chased her. Every once in a while she'd show a faint interest, allowing him to groom her. Then she'd go right back to ignoring him.

Sapolsky did some research and found several scientific experiments that went a long way toward explaining why Jonathan (like his many human counterparts) didn't just give up in the face of blatant rejection or indifference. In one of those, Wolfram Schultz at Switzerland's University of Fridbourg started by rewarding monkeys with food pellets every time they pressed a lever. While they did this, he monitored how much activity went on in the part of the frontal cortex that releases dopamine. He found the biggest burst happened before the monkeys got their pellets but after they'd pushed the lever. It peaked during the anticipation of the reward. That itself was interesting, but then Schultz, along with fellow researcher Christopher Fiorillo, went on to show that they could induce even more activity in the dopamine circuits when the rules were changed so that the monkeys had only a 50-percent chance of getting a treat.

Commenting on their work, Sapolsky reasoned that the animals' pleasure came from the anticipation coupled with the uncertainty. "At the worst end of it, it tells us about human addiction," he wrote. "At the best, it tells us what drives us to do challenging things." Which all seems to back up the Mystery Method and other pickup artists' tricks of the trade. From a woman's perspective, it's boring when a guy makes it too obvious from the start that you could hook a leash on him and walk him around the block. So these guys try to turn the tables by acting as cool as Rebecca.

This may sound simple, but for the men taking boot camp, it would require changing behavior patterns engrained over many years. From reading Neil Strauss's pickup manifesto, *The Game*, I learned that some men get drawn into a whole lifestyle built around seduction—a pickup culture. It seemed to me an extreme investment of energy just to get into women's pants.

Women seeking quick sex generally don't need to bother. Most books aimed at women try to help us extract commitment from men who may or may not already have had sex with us.

Why, then, are men but not women willing to work, to pay, to sweat, and to risk humiliation in order to achieve sex, even if there's no prospect of a real relationship? Evolutionary psychologists offer a piece of the explanation: Males in many species, including ours, invest less in reproduction. In those cases the males may invest more up front to get sex, while females experience the work and risk later, in being pregnant or rearing young or laying and incubating eggs. Of course, men aren't necessarily conscious of this when they're planning their pickup lines. It seems to come from instinct. But why? Did nature make sex better for males?

Maybe for some. In her 2006 book *I'd Rather Eat Chocolate*, author Joan Sewell admits she doesn't want sex more than twice a month with her frustrated, horny, and, she claims, very cute husband. According to a recent study out of Germany, Sewell and her many female fans are not alone. The German researchers found that both men and women desire sex equally at the start of a long-term relationship; but after twenty years, 60 to 80 percent of men still reported wanting sex regularly, while only 20 percent of women still did.

In Greek mythology, the goddess Hera and the god Zeus once made a bet over who gets the greater joy from sex. Hera bet that men enjoyed sex more. Zeus went with women. Eventually, they consulted a man named Tiresias, who had some special insight into the matter, as he had been magically transformed into a woman for seven years and then turned back into a man. In some accounts this all took place because he hit a pair of copulating snakes with a stick. Having seen love from both sides, Tiresias said he liked sexual intercourse much more when he was a she, thus winning the bet for Zeus and angering Hera so much she struck him blind.

The bet might have gone differently had they found a being that was simultaneously half male and half female and asked him/her which half liked sex more. That's not so hard to do if you're willing to look to some rather exotic animals. Flatworms go both ways, as do earthworms, slugs, and many snails. They're called simultaneous hermaphrodites because they can play male and female roles at the same time, as opposed to animals that change sex, like Tiresias.

EVERYBODY WANTS TO BE THE MALE

So what happens when boy/girl meets girl/boy? For help I went to biologist Nico Michiels of the University of Tübingen, Germany, who studies these sorts of creatures. He explained that simultaneous hermaphrodites often engage in a brutal combat over who gets to be the boy. In their battles over who assumes the male position, many resort to stabbing, drugging, or even chemical weapons. Take *Pseudoceros bifurcus*, a little sea worm that lives on Australia's Great Barrier Reef. When two of these meet, they start trying to stab each other with their penises. Whichever one gets stabbed first is fertilized and thereby becomes the de facto female. "Both are trying to stab the other without being stabbed," Michiels said. "Everybody wants to be the male."

That happens because these animals must contend with sexual conflict—a predicament in which what's good for one sex may harm the other one. That takes an unusual twist when everyone is both male and female. Whenever it's easier to give up sperm than to deposit eggs (usually because sperm are smaller), a hermaphrodite may succeed in the evolution game better as a he than a she. As explained in the first two chapters, the sperm, being smaller, are cheaper to make and so tend to proliferate and far outnumber the more expensive eggs. The more crowded a species' environment, the cheaper sperm get and the more aggressively males try to unload them. The bottom can really drop out of the sperm market when a creature's female side can store someone else's sperm. Then nobody wants to buy sperm and everybody wants to sell. And that can make the sellers aggressive.

In the polyclad flatworm, another sea-dwelling invertebrate, males squirt corrosive semen that burns holes in the flesh of other flatworms. When two of them engage in battle, the loser ends up not only pregnant but covered in big burns. "It can be quite severe," Michiels observed. In one of his scientific papers, Michiels described an even dirtier tactic employed by the tiny yellow sea slugs that live on the Great Barrier Reef. They try to stab each other with penises that inject an anesthetic. Once a stab is achieved, the winner's male side has sex with the loser's female side while he/she's under the influence of this built-in date-rape drug. "It's a very interesting system, because it's never clear beforehand which one will win," Michiels said. In this animal, "the penis is heavily armed with hooks and spines, and it anchors itself in the female genital tract." In that case, maybe it's a good thing the de facto female is anesthetized.

In creatures that can only assume one sex or the other, he said, the female could just run away if she didn't want to be stabbed or burned or drugged, but in these hermaphrodites her male half won't let her leave, so intent is he on doing the same deed to the other one's female side. Like the single human body shared by Steve Martin and Lily Tomlin in the movie *All of Me,* the male and female sides don't want the same thing.

Occasionally the tables turn. In other slug species, females have the power to reject a male after sex by rerouting the sperm to her stomach. That can shift the evolutionary pressure to favor males who are more reluctant to give up their precious bodily fluids. And that favors females with countermeasures. In one worm species, the female wields a penis-like organ that stabs the male, pokes a hole in him, and uses the appendage like a straw to "suck the sperm out," Michiels said. It's the animal version of the mythological succubus—a beautiful female demon who seduces men in order to suck the energy and life force from them.

Biologists say that sexual conflict becomes most intense when males don't invest much in either making sperm or nurturing babies. For males, that can turn sex into an evolutionary free lunch—you pass on your genes at little cost to you. Could such a scenario describe us?

For eons men enjoyed the biological prerogative to give up nothing beyond a few sperm, forcing all the work of childbearing onto the female. Under those circumstances, sex with the wrong man could prove disastrous for a woman. So perhaps a long evolutionary history of sexual conflict led Sewell and a certain number of other women to a preference for chocolate over sex. On the other hand, the rules of the game are changing fast. Contraceptives have given women control over our fertility, thus making sex more attractive to us, while DNA paternity testing makes it harder for males to get that free lunch. So perhaps it's only a matter of time before some guy comes out with *I'd Rather Drink Beer*.

If that happens, women may get more sex-crazed. The more one side grows blasé or picky or mean or cannibalistic, the more determined the other side must become in order to procreate. Neither sex has to enjoy the act of mating, but at least one party has to want it and put some effort into getting it.

Most of the so-called sex on television and in advertising doesn't depict copulation, after all, but just sexy people posed to trigger desire. It's all about the wanting, the chase, the competition. He who scores passes his genes on to the future. And that drives the evolution of our sex differences.

5. THE GENETICS OF MEN

HOW THE Y CHROMOSOME CAME ABOUT AND WHAT IT TELLS US ABOUT THE FUTURE OF MEN

Human sex differences begin with the Y chromosome—the only part of our genetic inheritance that's exclusively male. Despite much popular press surrounding the Y, it remains badly misunderstood as headlines often proclaim it's shrinking, or that it will disappear, or that it holds genes that make men superior to women. Luckily, biologists are in the process of deconstructing the Y, decoding its message and tracing how and when it evolved. That work is uncovering a new story about the origins of men and women and our various differences.

To tell the new story, I'll first dispense with some old mythology. In late 2006 an article ran in the magazine *American Spectator* under the brazen title, "Men Invented Humanity." The writer, William Tucker, credited this lofty achievement to the Y chromosome.

As evidence for the claim that men invented humanity, Tucker introduced what was then the latest comparison between the genetic codes of humans and chimpanzees. To bring his point home, he highlighted a single sentence from a *Time* magazine article on evolution and this latest chimp/human analysis: "First, they learned that overall, the sequence of base pairs that make up both species' [chimp's and human's] genomes differ by 1.23%—a ringing confirmation of the 1970 estimate—and that the most striking divergence between them occurs, intriguingly, in the Y chromosome, present only in males."

Subsequent research nudged the total chimp-human divergence a little higher yet backed up the fact that most of those differences did lie on the Y. But what does that really say about men and women? Tucker interpreted this to mean that women haven't evolved as much as men from our ape ancestors. Women, he wrote, just take care of babies, like chimp moms, while presumably men do all that important human stuff like build civilizations. But Tucker didn't explain what exactly was on the human Y chromosome that equipped men alone to invent humanity, or even how their Y chromosomes had diverged from those of the chimp males. Would scientists find genes for art, architecture, farming, and reasoning on the Y chromosome? Would they find anything to give women Y envy?

As a quick review, the chromosomes are microscopic islands of DNA that reside in nearly all of your billions of cells, and carry your genetic code. In human beings, both men and women have twenty-two pairs of chromosomes, named by the numbers one through twenty-two. Women have an additional pair, called the X chromosomes, and men have a mismatched pair—an X and a Y. So the Y represents the one part of the genetic code that really is unique to men. But is it responsible for the invention of humanity?

The human Y is just a nub of a chromosome, carrying only around eighty genes, as compared to more than a thousand on the X chromosome. In recent years most of the news about the Y made it look less than enviable. In his book *Adam's Curse,* geneticist Bryan Sykes called the Y a graveyard of rotting genes, a mess, a genetic ruin, and a wasteland littered with molecular wreckage that's crumbling before our eyes. Further tarnishing the reputation of the mighty Y is new evidence that it's not the rugged individualist it once appeared. The Y chromosome can't make a male on its own but relies on dozens of genes located on other chromosomes. A defect in one of these other genes can lead a person carrying a Y to look indistinguishable from a woman, or a person carrying two X's to look for all the world like a man.

Our sex-determining system relies on so many different genes because of the convoluted way it evolved—building on top of other sex-determining systems in other ancestral animals. Once the two separate sexes appeared, some 600 million years ago, living things invented a whole slew of different ways to separate the males from the females. Some employed genes to do the job. Others let some cue from the environment trigger either male or female development. In many reptiles, for example, the temperature at which an egg is incubated will determine its sexual fate.

Biologists are still piecing together the complex interplay of genes that makes some of us male and others female. It's a little like gathering clues to the Da Vinci Code, each new one adding to a tantalizing story of how our own system works—and how it evolved—as our ancestral line went from fish to amphibian to reptile to mammal.

Y chromosomes were discovered originally in mealworms. Geneticists Nettie Stevens and Edmund Beecher Wilson made the findings independently and published them in 1905. Back then, scientists were just beginning to connect the inheritance of traits to these strange microscopic filaments that showed up in cells when stained with dyes. The scientists called them chromosomes—Greek for "colored bodies."

Much confusion followed about whether humans had a Y and whether or not it determined maleness. In fruit flies and some other insects most males have a Y, though it isn't the deciding factor for sex. Some unusual flies have two X's and a Y, and they come out female, while others get just a single X with no Y, and they appear male. For fruit flies, it's the number of X chromosomes that determines sex, the females getting two and the males just one.

But the human Y is different, and its more critical role started to crystallize in the 1960s, when English scientists working on human genetics published a paper about a twenty-four-year-old man with an extra X chromosome. Unlike the XXY flies, which were female, this man was clearly a male. Men with one or more extra X chromosomes have what's called Klinefelter's syndrome, which causes infertility and other health problems such as atrophied testicles and development of breast tissue. But they are male.

Bolstering the case that our Y really did determine maleness was the discovery of women with what's called Turner's syndrome. These women carry just one X—no second X or Y, giving them one fewer chromosome than most people. They're usually infertile and sometimes report other problems, but they are clearly female. In humans, it became apparent the tiny Y mattered quite a bit.

Most mammals share an XY system similar to ours, but in birds it's the female who carries the Y chromosome, though by convention scientists call it a W, and the bird version of the X chromosome they call a Z. So female birds are WZ and males are ZZ. Reptiles show a whole variety pack of sex-determining systems. Snakes and some lizards use the WZ system of birds, while others use an X and Y system similar to mammals. Crocodiles, alligators, some turtles, and some lizards lack any genetic distinction between sexes, leaving it up to external factors. In diamondback terrapins, for example, if the temperature of an egg exceeds 84°F at some critical stage in development, it will emerge female. If below, it will be male.

But there are hazards to letting the weather determine the sex of our offspring. Your whole species can lose out in a drastic climate change. In the 1990s, turtle expert James Spotila and paleontologist Peter Dodson published a paper speculating that temperature had determined the sex of the dinosaurs—to their peril. Sixty-five million years ago, when, according to prevailing theory, a meteor struck and darkened the skies, global cooling could have led to many generations with no females. Males would be forced to mate with the dwindling ranks of females among the older generations. If that was the case, said Spotila, "The last dinosaur was one frustrated male."

Nobody knows for sure why the dinosaurs died and so many other species lived, but we do know that one of the survivors was the predecessor of the human Y chromosome, carried out of whatever disaster killed the dinosaurs in the cells of some scurrying, rodent-like mammal.

THE EXCEPTIONS THAT REVEALED THE RULE

Once scientists figured out that the Y was important for human beings and other mammals, they started racing to figure out just what the Y did that made men male. In the 1960s and seventies, they were turning up people who seemed to carry the wrong sex chromosomes in their cells. There were women with XY and men with XX, some of them unaware of anything out of the ordinary until they sought treatment for infertility.

These exceptional cases suggested that you didn't need a whole Y chromosome to be a male.

Studying XX men, scientists discovered that most of them carried small fragments of the Y that had become detached and then reattached to the X or some other chromosome. They reasoned that a key gene must lie in these fragments. Researchers also found that many XY women were missing parts of their Y, or carried mutations in these Y's. These women presumably carried impotent Y chromosomes, lacking in the part crucial to becoming male.

In 1990, British geneticists Peter Goodfellow and Robin Lovell-Badge announced they'd found a single maleness gene, which they called SRY for "sex-determining region on the Y." It was the only one of the eighty-some genes on the Y chromosome that really did the job. The Brits backed up their finding by injecting the gene into fertilized XX mouse eggs—otherwise destined to develop as females. The SRY gene alone turned these XX mice into males, and when Goodfellow and Lovell-Badge published their finding in *Nature*, the British journal ran a cover picture showing one of these genetically engineered SRY mice, legs apart, proudly displaying his testicles.

When I called Lovell-Badge at MRC National Institute for Medical Research in London, he told me the SRY played just a bit role in making a male, though it did get on stage first. "SRY is a typical male gene," he said. "It sleeps most of the time, then wakes up for a few hours, gives some instructions, and goes back to sleep again." The hard work of making males is done by other genes on the chromosomes shared by both males and females.

The central and seemingly most pivotal gene in making men male, he said, is called SOX9. It's on chromosome 17—one of the twenty-two pairs shared by both men and women. But in a male fetus, SRY sends a signal to SOX9. That prompts it to start transforming cells in the fetus's developing genital zone. SOX9 orchestrates the creation of what are called sertoli cells, which then go on to form testicles. Then hormones secreted by the tiny testes go on to masculinize the rest of the body. In some animals, heat changes the activity of SOX9, which explains how turtles could use temperature to determine sex.

Even without the rest of the Y chromosome, a detached SRY clinging to some other chromosome can flip the necessary genetic switches to start the development of a male. But until very recently the scientific consensus was that a person had to have at least an SRY gene to be fully male; that was until 2006, when they came across a very unusual family.

In an Italian village, two cousins married and bore eight sons and no daughters. Four of the sons were infertile and suffered from a congenital skin disease called palmoplantar hyperkeratosis as well as a predisposition to skin cancer. Genetic tests revealed these four brothers each had two X chromosomes and no SRY or any other piece of a Y.

It turned out those brothers would have been four sisters if not for a spelling error in another gene on chromosome 1 called R-spondin1, which nobody had ever connected to sex. The parents were carriers, in that they had just one misspelled copy of that gene. The four XX brothers each inherited two bad copies of R-spondin1. The other four brothers had Y chromosomes, so they were genetically destined to be male. "It was a fantastic piece of detective work," said Lovell-Badge.

It was a finding that called into question one of those old and often-repeated assumptions about maleness that many of us take for granted. For years, Lovell-Badge said, geneticists assumed that the default state for an embryo was to develop into a female. Lots of genes had to be activated to turn it into a male, the thinking went, such that if anything went wrong in this active male pathway, the fetus would revert to female.

But there in Italy, in 2006, scientists were looking at genetic females with a mutation that had caused them to revert to maleness. According to the scientific papers describing them, these XX men had normal testes and other male organs and they looked and acted like men. How could this be? Geneticists say it reveals that ovaries, too, are built by an active process that can break down. So there is no true "default" sex. If you think of SOX9 as a sex-determining faucet, the male SRY gene turns it on early in development. But if there's no SRY, the faucet still comes on at a trickle. Lovell-Badge suspects that in women, R-spondin1 gets up and turns off the leaky faucet. If it fails to do this, the faucet keeps leaking and the fetus develops as a male.

If the Y isn't even necessary in making a male, could it still carry anything on it that allowed men to invent humanity? Could these XX men be lacking that certain something? Research into the Y shows most of the genes there do nothing, though a few work in the sperm-making field, while at least one gene influences height— explaining why XY women are, on average, taller than XX women. The Y also carries genes that control tooth enamel, and researchers find unusually large teeth in men with an extra Y chromosome— XYY men. Such men used to be considered at high risk of delinquency and incarceration but subsequent research showed this was not true. Most men with an extra Y never know it.

The one gene on the Y that does work in the brain is the male-determining gene itself—SRY. Researchers working jointly in California and Australia announced in 2006 that in addition to switching on male development and then going to sleep, this maleness gene goes to work in part of the brain called the substantia nigra, which deteriorates in patients with Parkinson's disease. UCLA's Eric Villain said that in the brain, SRY influences the balance of a critical substance—dopamine—which is involved in pleasure, addiction, and movement. Women apparently regulate dopamine slightly differently, and the bad news for men is that the female mechanism appears less prone to trouble. Men are more likely to suffer from dopamine-related diseases, including addictions, schizophrenia, and Parkinson's disease.

WHAT WOULD JESUS' DNA DO?

When twentieth-century science revealed that most human males carry a unique male chromosome—the Y—it gave some men a point of pride, but it also posed a small problem for those believing in the world's most famous alleged Virgin Birth.

Did Jesus have a Y chromosome, and if so, where did it come from? His mother? The question of Jesus' biology entered public discourse following Dan Brown's fictional allegations in *The Da Vinci Code* and more recently, when a physicist named Frank Tipler tackled the issue in his book *The Physics of Christianity*. In a whole chapter devoted to Jesus' chromosomes, Tipler claimed that the Virgin Mary had a genetic abnormality that allowed her to give birth to a male child using only her own eggs—no sperm required.

When I wrote about Jesus' DNA for my newspaper column, many readers accused me of posing a stupid question. If God can do anything, they scolded, of course He can make Jesus a Y chromosome, or even an entire genetic code from scratch. God doesn't have to follow the laws of biology, these readers told me.

But when I floated the question to members of the theology community, I found many who took the issue seriously. Most told me Jesus was not a supernatural being. Responding to my query via e-mail, Georgetown University professor of theology John Haught wrote that the doctrine of incarnation says Jesus is fully human. "To imply that Jesus is somehow exempt from ordinary natural laws and biological patterns (including having DNA and male chromosomes) would, in my view, be a failure to take the incarnation seriously."

Some nevertheless took the view that God must have fashioned at least part of Jesus' DNA Himself, through a miracle. "It's not God's sperm. . . . But God created something like a sperm and caused it to fertilize Mary's egg," said Ron Cole-Turner, a professor and ordained minister at the Pittsburgh Theological Seminary. Biology professor David Wilcox of Eastern University, a Christian college in Pennsylvania, said some aspects of reality may lie beyond the reach of science. "Of course Jesus had DNA and a Y chromosome— and the source for half of that DNA (and the Y chromosome) would presumably be a pure and simple miracle," he said.

If that's the case, maybe there's reason to feel uneasy about the premise of The Da Vinci Code, that Jesus had sex with Mary Magdalene and let his DNA loose into the general population.

But other Christian thinkers said the Virgin Birth is a misinterpretation. "There's a big split over the Y chromosome issue," said

Boston University theology professor Wesley Wildman. Wildman said it's not as big a problem for Protestants like him to accept a nonvirgin Mary as it is for Catholics, who revere her. The Bible itself is ambiguous on the point, he said, since it contains the prophesy that an *almah* will give birth to the Messiah, and *"alma"* can mean virgin or young girl.

Natural conception was problematic to early Christian thinkers, Wildman said, because Augustine and others taught that original sin was passed on "through the male via the loss of control associated with male orgasm." That's why Catholic theologians introduced the concept of Immaculate Conception, he said. It's a term often misunderstood as the conception of Jesus, but it really refers to the conception of Mary herself. Mary's mother need not have been a virgin but somehow God blocked the passing of original sin.

Wildman said that as a Protestant theologian he has no trouble accepting that Joseph was the biological father of Jesus. But Tulane University physicist Tipler takes yet a third view, which he explains in *The Physics of Christianity*.

Tipler maintains that miracles do occur, and while they may seem to be vastly improbable, they don't break the laws of physics or biology. In this vein Tipler goes about explaining how Jesus could have been born a male—a miracle that takes considerably more space to explain than the simple matter of Mary giving birth as a virgin.

His hypothesis: that Mary carried a genetic anomaly. She had bits of the Y chromosome stuck in her X chromosome, just as scientists have found in most XX males. As long as such people carry a fragment of the Y with the key male-determining gene—the

SRY—they turn out male. And that poses a small problem. If Mary had an SRY she would most likely be a man, and if she lacked an SRY, then Jesus should have been a woman.

To deal with that, Tipler proposes that through another rare genetic anomaly, Mary's SRY was suppressed and then reactivated in her son. It may be astronomically unlikely, said Tipler, but in his view Mary had not just an inactive SRY but all the rest of the Y chromosome genes lurking in her X.

Scientists don't have any known cases of a suppressed SRY in a human female that was later reactivated. However, something like that has been seen in four species of South American vole mice. In her book *Evolution's Rainbow*, biologist Joan Roughgarden notes that in these species, "15 to 40 percent of females have both SRY and a Y chromosome, yet they are still female and make eggs."

So Tipler's proposed series of genetic anomalies could happen, in theory. It's just very unlikely, up there with all the readers of this book winning more than a million dollars in the lottery tomorrow. And then another rare anomaly would be needed to bring about a virgin birth—since that, too, has never been documented in a human being.

A simpler possibility would be that Jesus had a genetic defect similar to the one seen in those four XX brothers in Italy. That defect could in theory produce males with no male-generated genes. Mary could have carried a single mutation in R-spondin1 and a second mutation could have hit the self-fertilized egg that went on to become Jesus. The Italian brothers with this defect, from all accounts, looked and acted fully male except they couldn't make any sperm. That would render unlikely the *Da Vinci Code* premise that Jesus himself procreated. Whether Tipler's idea gets taken seriously may depend on the willingness of Christians to embrace the idea of Jesus as a genetic anomaly.

THE SHRINKAGE OF THE Y

All these anomalies reveal the flexibility of our genetics. We carry the latent potential in each of us to develop as either sex. In the future, we may need to rely on that flexibility if rumors of the Y going extinct turn out to be true. Those rumors are based on a controversial scientific theory widely reported in the popular press a few years back. If it turns out to be true, then to keep the human race from dying out we'd need to quickly evolve a new way to make males.

David Page, a geneticist at the Whitehead Institute in Massachusetts, said he expects the Y to hang around a while longer. The key to its future, he said, lies in understanding the Y's past. His analysis, as he explained it to me, shows the Y chromosome evolved from an X. The Y shares just enough common stretches of genetic code with the X to give away this pair's ancient relationship. It all started some 300 million years ago, said Page, in some lizard-like reptile that used temperature or some other system to separate the sexes. Both sexes of this ancestral reptile had two X chromosomes, but one day a mutation struck a gene on the X chromosome. That mutation automatically turned any lizard who inherited it into a male. The acquisition of this new gene, whatever it was, started this X chromosome on the road to becoming a Y. Because the nascent Y had the power to turn any animal possessing it male, the chromosome started accumulating other genes that benefited males.

Page said after all these years the Y and X still share eighteen common genes—a relic of the Y's past as an X. On the Y, those eighteen unused genes have been accumulating typos at a known rate since they stopped getting swapped back and forth with the X, he said. Counting those typos gave him the estimate of 300 million years for the birth of the Y that human beings inherited. Since then, the Y inherited by mankind has shrunk. Under the microscope it looks stunted compared to the X and carries fewer than 10 percent of its original complement of genes.

Why did the Y get so small? To answer this, it might help to revisit our relatives the chimps, whose Y chromosome is even smaller than the human one. Page was one of the scientists who collaborated on the chimp-human comparison referenced in Tucker's article "Men Invented Humanity." It is indeed true, Page said, that the biggest difference between the two species is on the Y. But he draws a different conclusion from Tucker. Humans did not evolve from chimps—both species, and their respective Y chromosomes, branched off from a common ancestor between 5 and 8 million years ago. Since then, chimps have continued to evolve, becoming more chimplike. Page said our Y is more stable than the chimp's Y. It's changed relatively little since that split, while the chimp Y has lost dozens of genes and become ultraspecialized in sperm production. The best explanation for this, according to Page, involves the radical sexual habits of chimp females, who sometimes try to mate with as many males as possible when they come into heat. And they move fast: female chimps have been seen mating with eight males in less than fifteen minutes. "That puts intense pressure for males to produce great volumes of sperm," Page said.

So in chimps, where sperm count is all important, garbled versions of the more general Y chromosome genes rode along with the good sperm-making ones. The pressure on the chimp to produce sperm caused its Y to overlook quality control, said Page. Sometimes mutations called "deletions" would simply erase out a gene. Over time those deletions caused the Y to get physically smaller than the X.

Since the chimps split off from our lineage, said Page, their Y has eroded faster than the human one and has hoarded more sperm-enhancing genes. The result: a chimp boasts testicles twice the size of a man's and a sperm count that makes ours look dismal, said Page. Sorry guys, but it appears that the big divergence between human and chimp Y chromosomes didn't necessarily help you invent humanity. It gave chimps bigger balls.

BAD NEWS FROM WEIRD ANIMALS

How much more will it shrink? The long-term prognosis for the Y chromosome depends on who you ask. Page is optimistic about it, but geneticist Jenny Graves of the Australian National University says the human Y is doomed.

Graves was the first one to make this gloomy forecast, which she reached after studying what she calls the "weird" animals. One of the weirdest—the duck-billed platypus—lives on her continent of Australia. It's a warm-blooded, milk-producing mammal but it slithers on alligator-like hind limbs and the females lay eggs. It's a member of a small class of mammals called the monotremes, which branched off early from other mammalian lineages some 200 million years ago. Later, the marsupials such as the kangaroo and opossum branched off from our line, the placental mammals.

In 2004, Graves and colleagues discovered that a male platypus has five Y chromosomes and five X chromosomes. A female has ten X chromosomes. It's a system that she thought looked needlessly complex. Nobody could quite figure out how it worked until scientists finished sequencing the entire genetic code of the platypus in 2007.

The big surprise, said Graves, was that none of the males' Y chromosomes carried the critical gene, the SRY, that determines maleness in almost all other mammals. The male platypus's Y's are not related to ours, she said. Instead of SRY on the Y, the platypus has a gene called DRT1 on the X chromosomes. This is a gene she believes determines sex in birds.

In birds, the sex chromosomes are called W and Z, and the females get the mismatched pair, one Z and one W, while males get two Z's. That's what she refers to as the "chickenoid system," named after one of the most closely studied birds.

"It's very strange," said Graves. And with five X's and five Y's, sex, at least at the cellular level, looks like a very difficult sorting act. Offspring must get exactly five Y chromosomes or none to survive. "It seems like a stupid way of doing things, but it works," she said, which is all that matters for survival.

But how would such a thing evolve in the first place? The most likely story is that a common ancestor to the platypus and all other mammals used the same sex-determining scheme as the chicken. The platypus, Graves said, inherited "a chickenoid system that went slightly berserk." Various ordinary chromosomes got dragged into the role of sex chromosomes, she said.

The chickenoid system of W and Z chromosomes looks to be very ancient, she said. What's interesting in comparing birds and mammals is that our human chromosome 9 shares some elements with the chicken Z, suggesting a common evolutionary origin for the 9 and Z. Conversely, the chicken chromosomes 1 and 4 share stretches of genes with our X.

What does the platypus have to do with the human Y? The weirdness of the platypus genetics suggests that the human Y emerged after the platypus branched off from other mammals, around 200 million years ago. That means our Y is younger than was thought, she said. And if the human Y is younger, then it must have been degenerating faster to have reached its present shrunken state. In Graves' estimate, the human Y chromosome is going extinct in 10 million years.

Graves said she's constantly surprised at the reaction she gets from men when she tells them the Y is going away. "Ten million years is a long time," she said, considering that human beings have existed not even a million years. "But nevertheless men feel very threatened by this." It's a common misconception that men will become extinct at that point, she said. People assume that somehow women will evolve the ability to reproduce without sperm. But that's difficult for mammals, she said.

In the event that humans somehow do survive another 10 million years, she said, we might experience a fate similar to that of the mole vole. Males of that species have no Y chromosomes, and since all their close relatives do, it appears they used to have one but lost it. And yet, the mole voles keep having babies that come out about fifty-fifty males and females, so some new male-determining mechanism must have taken over.

Something similar happened in another species of vole, as well as in a Y-less Japanese country rat. All these animals either reverted to an earlier system for sex determination or they evolved some new switch. Maleness goes much deeper into evolutionary history than the Y chromosome. If these other mammals can live without it, so can we. When it comes to sex, nature is nothing if not creative.

6. PRIVATE PARTS

EVERYTHING YOU EVER WANTED
TO KNOW ABOUT PHALLOLOGY

Before the discovery of the human Y chromosome in the mid-twentieth century, the primary symbol and totem of manhood was the penis. The organ of sexual intercourse served as the primary distinguisher of the sexes. Sigmund Freud placed the phallus at the center of man's unconscious mind. But how did it evolve and what does it really say about the way the sexes differ?

If I had to learn all about the penis, what better place to start my research than Iceland, home to the world's only penis museum—the Institute of Phallology. By coincidence, my newspaper sent me to Iceland in 2006 to report on a company that specialized in human genetics. Since I also write about sex, I added the penis museum to my itinerary.

I hoped the museum would allow me to see this seemingly simple organ stripped of some of the mystery, confusion, and hype that people have attached to it over the ages. The penis has been misdrawn, misrepresented, misinterpreted, and misunderstood more than any other body part, save, perhaps, for the vagina.

I'd always been taught that the penis was among those "private parts," and it's not just prudish Americans who keep their members clothed. Men in most cultures cover their genitalia, possibly out of instinct, say anthropologists. Since a man's genitalia represent his one shot at passing on his genes, natural selection may have bred in men a desire to keep it safe. If you're spending your days hunting in a rain forest somewhere, it might serve your best interests to protect your penis and testicles from brush, nettles, poison ivy, snakes, mosquitoes, ticks, leeches, and various other threats.

That's why man has devised so many interesting varieties of penis belts, penis gourds, and loincloths. Sometimes they're designed with an eye toward modesty, other times decorated and built up to accentuate masculinity, as happened with the ground-skimming penis gourds that became fashionable in New Guinea.

Perhaps it was this longstanding habit of covering these things up that was making me reluctant to tell my boyfriend, who'd accompanied me to Iceland, about our plans to see the penis museum. When I finally brought it up, he suggested we go on a whale-watching tour instead. His enthusiasm was diminished further when I finally reached the place by phone and discovered it had moved from the cosmopolitan capital city of Reykjavik, where we were staying, to the remote northern coast of Iceland.

The man who answered the phone said that, indeed, the museum had moved in 2004 to Husavik, a fishing village, population 2,500, located on a northern peninsula jutting to within a few miles of the Arctic Circle. On the map, Husavik appeared almost as hard to reach from whichever direction you set out on the single highway that traced the country's perimeter. You can't cut through the middle of Iceland, which is covered in rocky hills, lava flows, and glaciers. So we would drive full circle. To my relief, my boyfriend liked the notion of circumnavigating Iceland by rental car, and I made sure to impart how much I'd need his help on this long and possibly dangerous adventure. But when I called the museum one last time to get directions once we reached Husavik, the man who answered said, "Just ask anyone." It was one thing having to navigate 300 miles of semipaved roads that hairpin around Iceland's tortured landscape, another to ask complete strangers how to find a penis museum.

Luckily, at the end of two days of driving we needed no help finding the museum, since it was marked by a giant carved phallus rising up on the front yard like an X-rated totem pole. The name "Institute of Phallology" suggested corridors of scientists dissecting penises and students completing advanced degrees in phallology. But it was really just the private collection of a retired history teacher named Sigurdur Hjartarson. The day we arrived, the museum was open by appointment only, as it was most days, so Mr. Hjartarson met us at the door and gave us a personal tour. The sixty-four-year-old father of four had collected more than 240 specimens—all obtained from animals that had already expired, so none were killed for his display. There were stuffed whale penises the length of fencing foils, pickled penises floating in jars, dried fibrous penises and penis bones. The biggest specimen was a five-foot-two-inch organ once belonging to a sperm whale and now preserved in a cylinder of formaldehyde. It was twice as long when it was still attached to the whale, explained Hjartarson.

He told us he started collecting penises the same way others collect frogs or rubber ducks. Back in the 1970s, he said, a colleague with a summer job at a nearby whaling station brought him a whale penis as a curiosity. Soon others, thinking he was a collector, brought him more. Now he owns specimens from around the world, including representatives of every mammal currently living in Iceland—except for the human being (and that was to change soon, as several men, including one ninety-one-year-old Icelander, had willed their members to the museum).

"Phallology" is more likely to be practiced as part of other disciplines, such as biology, but penis studies trace an illustrious history. One of the world's first phallologists was Saint Augustine, the early Christian philosopher known for his saying "Lord, give me chastity, but not yet." In the early fifth century A.D. he expounded on the trouble with penises in his work *The City of God*. "At times, the urge intrudes uninvited. At other times, it deserts the panting lover and, although desire blazes in the mind, the body is frigid." In a fascinating natural history of the penis called *A Mind of Its Own*, author David Friedman details Augustine's struggles with the male organ and the esteemed theologian's explanation for its waywardness: God took away man's control of his own erections as a punishment for Adam's defiant tasting of the forbidden fruit. Ever since that fateful transgression, Augustine wrote, original sin passed down through the generations via semen. Thus the penis became the instrument of original sin.

A more scientific phallologist was Leonardo da Vinci, who revolutionized humanity's understanding of the body through art and dissection in the late fifteenth and early sixteenth centuries. According to Friedman's penis book, other medical men of his time thought an erection was kept stiff by air pressure. Da Vinci argued, correctly, that it was made stiff by blood. He based his idea partly on the reddish color he saw in the head of the erect penis— something he said he observed by studying hanged criminals, whose members apparently became engorged.

One of the world's most prominent phallologists today is a

woman by the name of Diane Kelly, who works in the Biology Department at the University of Massachusetts, Amherst. What fascinates her about the penis, she told me, is the way it evolved independently in different animals, just as wings evolved separately in birds, insects, and bats. It's not known how many times the penis was reinvented by evolution—perhaps four or five in land vertebrates alone. Among reptiles, birds, and mammals, she said, "each lineage has a very different kind of penis," and evolution came up with many ways to erect them. Birds use not blood but lymphatic fluid. Mammals use an internal balloon that fills with blood but also depends on two layers of collagen fibers that become stiff when the structure is inflated. That's the general plan for most mammals, she said, though it might work differently in the platypus. Nobody has yet documented the platypus penis.

A host of variations on this balloon theme grace the different mammals. Some, including cattle, antelopes, pigs, deer, elk, and moose, have what's called a "fibroelastic" penis, which stays semi-stiff all the time and is controlled primarily by muscles. (Augustine might conclude that these animals pleased the Lord as the system seems more failure-proof than ours.) Other animals, including human beings, have what's called a "vascular" penis, which relies more on the inflation of a spongy erectile tissue with blood.

Many of our vascular relatives get help from a penis bone, or baculum. Animals blessed with a penis bone include seals, walruses, mice, bats, chimpanzees, and polar bears. To quell any pangs of baculum envy, I should point out the major downside to this anatomical accessory: you can break your penis bone, as evidenced by an American opossum's broken and fused bone in the Institute of Phallology's collection. So the vulnerability to erectile dysfunction that Augustine viewed as a curse may have come about as an evolutionary trade-off. For us, evolution favored safety over reliability.

When we got through with the museum, my trusty male companion and I both decided it was worth the trip for educational value alone, though he thought it was a little too male-centric. "They should have a vagina museum somewhere," he said. Well, we do have *The Vagina Monologues,* at least. But is the vagina the true female counterpart of the penis? Or would that be the clitoris? To answer that question we'll need to delve into a little developmental biology.

WHY WOMEN HAVE PROSTATES

The most amazing and mind-boggling miracle of the penis, as well as the scrotum, testicles, prostate, and all the rest, is that it all appears so distinct from female genitalia, especially considering how little men and women differ genetically. As explained in chapter 5, it takes only a single gene on the Y chromosome, called SRY, to set a human embryo on a course toward maleness. And geneticists say the SRY doesn't really do that much except flip a switch early in development and then go to sleep.

Popular wisdom has long held that we all start life as females, but that's not quite the case. "You actually have the plumbing for both genders in early embryos," explained biologist Patricia Labosky, formerly of the University of Pennsylvania and now at Vanderbilt. At eight weeks, both males and females have a proto-penis and proto-prostate, as well as a proto-uterus and proto-vagina.

All of these proto-organs are unique in having what's called bipotentiality, said Scott Gilbert, a developmental biologist at Swarthmore College, near Philadelphia. Ordinarily, once cells start differentiating into a kidney or part of a lung, they can't change course. The sex organs are different. At eight weeks, the embryonic genitalia sit at a crossroads, waiting for genes to steer them in one direction or the other. If the embryo is to become a girl, what would have been the penis becomes its sister organ, the clitoris. So the female analogue of the penis is the clitoris, and it's the size of the organ that determines which name it gets. If doctors see something smaller than one centimeter in a newborn baby, they announce, "It's a girl." Conversely, the medical establishment has set the minimum penis size for a newborn boy at 2.5 centimeters. Though most babies do fit into one category or another, a significant number are born with organs somewhere between those two sizes.

What becomes the prostate in men also goes on to develop in women, becoming the sensitive glands that surround a woman's so-called G-spot and sometimes lend it erotic, orgasmic power. To learn more about this somewhat elusive female feature, I called G-spot guru Beverly Whipple, a professor emerita at Rutgers University College of Nursing in New Jersey. She tried to explain to me what you're supposed to look for—or feel for. Apparently, you're not seeking a special patch on the vaginal wall—you're trying to feel through the wall for something in the next room over. There you may encounter something that feels like a "spongy bean." The G-spot isn't really erotic in itself but a portal to an adjacent glandular universe.

The main feature of that universe was once known as the paraurethral glands, or Skenes glands, but in 2001 they were officially renamed the "female prostate" by the Federative International Committee on Anatomical Terminology. It now appears that some women get a more developed prostate than others, and for them, touching the prostate just the right way, via the G-spot, can induce them to ejaculate much the way men do.

As part of her studies, Whipple analyzed the whitish, semen-like fluid expelled by such gifted women and found that it's definitely not urine and shares some common ingredients with semen. Just as the male prostate produces the fluid that carries sperm to their various destinations, the female version sometimes creates an ejaculate if rubbed the right way. The phenomenon only seems baffling under the old "we all start out female" paradigm. It makes perfect sense with the understanding that we all begin life with the makings of both sexes.

Boy embryos, on the other hand, keep some of their girl parts, while actively destroying others, said Gilbert. The makings of the male plumbing are called Wolffian ducts (named after a certain Dr. Wolff), those of the female, Mullerian ducts (named after a certain Dr. Muller). In females, the Wolffian ducts degenerate without sufficient testosterone. In males, the testosterone from the developing testes causes the ducts to become the export tubes for the sperm.

A boy embryo makes not only testosterone but something called anti-Mullerian hormone, which goes to work demolishing the Mullerian ducts, preventing them from developing into the fallopian tubes, uterus, and upper part of the vagina. There's no anti-nipple hormone, however, so those stay with males. The lower part of the vagina also hangs around in males to become something called the prostatic utricle. It is a duct that, in the male, leads nowhere, said Gilbert.

As if our sexual anatomy weren't complex enough, nature made the male sex organ even more confusing by adapting it for an additional use in waste disposal. Leonardo da Vinci made one of his most famous anatomical errors in his depiction of the penis, equipping it with two urethras—one for urine and one for semen. It was as if the brilliant anatomist simply couldn't fathom the notion of God giving man just one tube for the passage of urine *and* the creation of new life.

Four centuries later, a concern with the proximity of elimination and sex seized James Holsinger, a Kentucky cardiologist who was nominated by George W. Bush in 2007 to become the next surgeon general. Almost immediately after his nomination, a quasi-scientific paper surfaced that Dr. Holsinger had written in 1991 for the United Methodist Church. Called "The Psychopathology of Male Homosexuality," its main point seemed to be that gay men shouldn't have anal sex (he waffled about its advisability for straights), but the paper revealed much more, especially about American's contemporary understanding of and attitude toward the penis.

It came as a surprise to many who read it how much lurid detail the Methodist Church seemed to want about the vulnerability of rectal epithelial cells and how the anus was "designed" as an exit. When Senator Ted Kennedy questioned Dr. Holsinger about it at a hearing, the main concern centered on the possible antigay prejudice voiced by our would-be surgeon general. And so, less attention was focused on what Holsinger wrote about human sex organs, which would have called into question his scientific understanding. "The structure and function of the male and female human reproductive systems are fully complementary," he wrote. "Anatomically the vagina is designed to receive the penis."

The fact that he used the word "designed" rather than "evolved" is enough to raise suspicion, but it's also telling that he didn't write the obverse—namely, that the penis was designed to be received by the vagina. His paper seemed to assume that the penis always existed, and that other body parts were designed around it. In defending himself before Kennedy, Dr. Holsinger said his paper was outdated, having been written in 1991. He was right about the outdated part: it would have been spot-on had he published it about 450 years earlier, when the best scientists of the day thought the vagina was designed for the penis. The most famous anatomist of the early to mid-1500s, Andreas Vesalius, drew an accurate representation of the penis but a gross distortion of the vagina, in which that organ looked like a penis turned inside out.

A LESSON FROM TWO STREET ACROBATS

To give credit to Dr. Holsinger, he wasn't able to include the first use of magnetic resonance imaging (MRI) to clarify what really went on with the penis and vagina during sexual intercourse. That feat was performed in the late 1990s in Holland, where it required the assistance of two street acrobats. Biologist Pek van Andel reported that he had been inspired by an MRI of a professional singer's vocal cords in action. That made him wonder what MRI technology could tell us about an act much more elemental and more common.

In press accounts, van Andel complained that he encountered constant heckling, yet he was following a line of inquiry that Leonardo da Vinci started in the late 1400s. As part of his anatomical studies, Leonardo drew a cross-sectional view of a copulating couple under the heading, "I expose to men the origin of their first, and perhaps second, reason for existing." Leonardo got a couple of things wrong, since he had to rely on his own imagination and the flawed understanding of anatomy and physiology of his time. Back then, doctors thought semen was manufactured in the brain and flowed down through the spinal column, for example. But surely if he had access to MRI, da Vinci would have jumped at the chance to check his picture against the real thing.

So starting where Leonardo left off, van Andel eventually recruited eight couples willing to have sex inside the machine. They had to be smaller than average, since both parties were required to squeeze themselves into the twenty-inch diameter tube and proceed to make love. Speaking through an intercom, a radiologist helping van Andel asked the couples to periodically stop the action for the "pictures."

Van Andel found, to his surprise, that men's penises really sprouted from long roots that extended far inside their bodies, and that once it entered a woman, the whole thing was contorted into the shape of a boomerang. That fact lent the resulting images a strange but touching symmetry, showing about half the boomerang inside the woman and the other half inside the man.

A cigar, then, is really just half of a phallic symbol. By highlighting the little-appreciated root that made up the other arm of the boomerang, van Andel greatly extended the estimate for the average erection length. Studies that used both self-reporting and clinical measurements placed that average between 5 and 5.35 inches. Van Andel's estimate boosted that to 8.7 inches.

The results were reported in the Christmas issue of the *British Medical Journal*, where van Andel expressed some surprise that so many of the male members of his couples had erection trouble once they crawled inside the confines of the machine. Only the first couple recruited succeeded without the help of a Viagra-type drug. Reporting in his journal article, van Andel speculated on that lone couple's success. "The reason might be . . . because of their scientific curiosity, knowledge of the body and artistic commitment. And as amateur street acrobats they are trained and used to performing under stress."

UNLUCKY DUCKS

If Dr. Holsinger is wrong and the vagina was not created to fit over a penis, then what really did happen according to the evolutionary picture? Biologists often look to other species for clues, and in doing so can't fail to notice that however it's measured, the human penis is much longer than that of most of our primate cousins, and certainly longer than it needs to be to accomplish the mission of injecting sperm into a woman. The mighty gorilla gets the job done with something little longer than an inch. One explanation is that fitting into the vagina represents just one item on the evolutionary agenda of the human penis. Some evolutionary theorists argue, for example, that it evolved its present size because our ancestors used it for display. In *The Mating Mind*, evolutionary psychologist Geoffrey Miller suggests that women kept choosing men with big ones just as peahens chose males with elaborate tails.

Other biologists note that many male animals need their penises not only to deliver sperm but to block, outcompete, or get rid of other sperm deposited earlier by their rivals. Why would females bother collecting sperm from different males? Traditionally, males were considered the more promiscuous sex, since the evolutionary advantage of male promiscuity is obvious—it spreads your genes around. But evolution also may favor females who cheat.

Often such behavior helps her beget offspring with healthier genes. If she's a member of a relatively monogamous species, she might get the chance to combine her genes with a better-looking, stronger male than her regular mate. Evolution favors males who can cope with this situation, which means avoiding being cuckolded. This term for infidelity derives from the cuckoo bird, the female of which has a reputation for clandestinely laying eggs in her neighbors' nests. Whether avian or human, males who pass on the most genes are those who can successfully avoid expending valuable time and energy bringing up another's brood, so many males have evolved anti-cuckolding traits.

For some very promiscuous species, such as chimpanzees, the best defense is often a high sperm count, which may explain why chimp testicles are nearly twice the size of a human's. Other male animals compete by acquiring the ability to scrape or pull out sperm from rivals. The penises of some creatures sport "spikes and knobs and bristles and are often twisted into weird and sinister shapes," writes biologist Olivia Judson in her book *Dr. Tatiana's Sex Advice to All Creation*. Sometimes the penis stays with the female. When the male honeybee mates with a queen, he leaves his penis stuck inside her, blocking entry for anyone else. Having achieved his highest possible goal in life, the rest of his body explodes.

Some animals deal with the threat of female infidelity by staying engaged in intercourse for excessive periods of time. The current record holder is the stick insect, according to John Alcock, an evolutionary biologist at Arizona State University. Stick insect sex can "go on for several months," he said. It's not clear this is welcome to the female stick insect. The male plants himself on the female's back and attaches himself there. Luckily for her, the male is about half her size. While clearly encumbered, she can still go about her business. For many species, Alcock said, "both sexes are quite capable of getting food while they are mating."

Male rats engage in a less deadly version of bee sex by leaving a "plug" to prevent other sperm from entering the female's reproductive tract. Once that tactic became widespread, other male rats evolved the ability to use their penises like plungers to remove the plug left by the rat who was there before. In the early 1990s, biologists Robin Baker and Mark Bellis suggested that humans evolved from a plug-leaving ancestor. That, they claimed, explains all that thrusting that goes on. "The repetitive motion was not designed to bring about female pleasure," they wrote. "It was intended to remove a competitor's soft plug and now functions as a piston-like pull-push-scrub-scrape mechanism."

Men may not be aware of it, but during sex they instinctively use their penises as "sperm displacement devices," said evolutionary psychologist Todd Shackelford of Florida Atlantic University, who followed up on Baker and Bellis. He and other enterprising scientists used plastic models of human sex organs to see if the old pull-push-scrub-scrape really worked to clean out leftover sperm. Apparently it does.

Human males may be endowed with bigger penises than they need, but they don't come close to the apparent excess of the duck. Though only 3 percent of bird species have a penis at all, ducks tend to have long and elaborate ones. The most egregious example is the Argentine lake duck, whose member stretches to fifteen-inches—longer than the rest of the duck. What leads evolution to favor such a thing? Usually it's very promiscuous females, said Patricia Brennan, a Yale University biologist who's been investigating duck genitalia. Sometimes a long penis helps a male compete with his rivals by either displacing sperm or getting his own sperm injected further into the female body and closer to the eggs.

Some ducks employ weird shapes as well as excessive length. A few have penises that twist like corkscrews. To investigate this phallological mystery, Brennan looked for clues in—where else?—duck vaginas. But what she found was even more baffling. "It spirals as well, but in the opposite direction as the male spiral," she said, which would appear to make sex difficult. Beyond that, she found duck vaginas often had pockets and cul-de-sacs. (If ducks could write creation stories, they'd probably attribute this to punishment from the great Duck God for eating of the forbidden weeds.)

After examining sixteen different duck species, she found that the longer penises went with longer vaginas. In a paper she published in early 2007, she suggested that the female's reproductive tract evolved to keep out the penises of undesirable males, which in many species have a habit of trying to force themselves on females who'd already chosen a different mate. A long, convoluted vagina with a reverse spiral would make it hard for a male to impregnate a female without her full cooperation. Brennan saw both sexes evolving in a kind of arms race. The males evolve longer penises because that helps them force sex on females. The females then evolve longer vaginas to foil the males. In response, the penises evolve to get longer still. Both sexes coevolve, adapting to gain control over their own reproduction at the expense of the other sex.

The corkscrew twists of the duck penises remain unexplained. How could this possibly benefit the males? Brennan said that as part of a follow-up investigation, she's hoping to coax male ducks to mate with an anatomically correct female decoy made from a transparent material, so she can see how the male's weird penis fits into the female's weird vagina. When I last spoke with her, she said that while the decoys are ready, the males hadn't yet started cooperating.

7. TESTOSTERONE

HOW TO MAKE A MAN, AND SOME THINGS
THAT CAN GO AWRY IN THE PROCESS

Men and women may seem to be at odds in our desires and in battle over our roles in society, but we're made from the same starting materials. And as we develop, we differ in most ways only as a matter of degree. This new view of the sexes emerged as science diminished the role of the Y chromosome, which is exclusively male, and discovered the central importance of testosterone, which both sexes share.

In humans, the Y chromosome is just the ignition key for maleness, while testosterone is its fuel. When a male fetus is just a few weeks along, biologists say the Y prompts the formation of male gonads, and it's up to those incipient testes to secrete hormones that do everything else—the first order of business being to create all those dangly bits known as external genitalia.

Women like Cindy Stone know firsthand that the Y alone can't make you a man. Stone, an administrator in the gender studies program at Indiana University, said she always looked and felt like a girl, and later a woman. Everyone else thought so, too. She never suspected anything unusual until she failed to menstruate. A doctor told her at seventeen that she had a birth defect and would never have children. She still assumed she was simply an infertile woman.

It wasn't until she was in her thirties that she got the whole story. She had a complete Y chromosome like any man, but a defect on another chromosome made it impossible for her body to react to testosterone. Her condition, she found, was called "compete androgen insensitivity syndrome." Six weeks into her development in utero, her Y chromosome (really a single gene on the Y) switched on, and prompted her then-neutral gonads to become testicles. Those began to make testosterone, which under normal circumstances would work to shape external male genitalia. But because of her syndrome, she lacked a critical protein that carries testosterone to the cell nucleus. It was as if her body was immune to it. Since she was developing inside a woman's uterus, she started to take her cues from her mother's female hormones, even though she was genetically male. She developed a vagina and in some ways came out more feminine than an ordinary woman. She had almost no body hair or acne, which other women get from our own small allotment of testosterone.

On average, we women have about a tenth as much testosterone as men; but, as I would come to learn, the amount individual men and women secrete varies wildly. When women who want to become men start injecting testosterone, the effect can be an almost magical transformation. Their voices deepen, muscles develop, fat redistributes itself, their head hair thins, and they grow beards. The obvious power of this hormone has encouraged humans to attach all kinds of value judgments to it. At one point, it was regarded as poison and blamed for all that was wrong with humanity. Later, it was credited with almost everything that's admirable.

Testosterone was discovered only relatively recently. Since men had been in the habit of castrating animals and their fellow men for years, they knew there was something important to masculinity that was secreted from testicles. That knowledge led more than a few men to consume ground-up testicles of various creatures. In Victorian England, monkey testes became popular as a male elixer to restore youth and virility. Still, nobody knew what the specific substance was until 1927, when University of Chicago chemist Fred Koch took advantage of his proximity to the Chicago stockyards to gather more than forty pounds of bull testicles, from which he extracted testosterone. He showed he'd indeed found the key substance by injecting it into castrated roosters and rats, which subsequently regained their potency and their sex drive.

The bad years for testosterone started around 1975. A new pejorative term, "testosterone poisoning," was reportedly coined that year by Alan Alda, who used it in an article for *Ms.* magazine. The term was bandied about through the 1980s and nineties, as it became conventional wisdom that testosterone was bad for behavior and bad for health. In his 2003 book *Y: The Descent of Men*, geneticist Steve Jones wrote that eunuchs tend to live longer than intact men, which he attributed to their having very low testosterone. Testosterone was blamed for male heart attacks, high blood pressure, and the general fact that men die younger than women. But by the start of the twenty-first century, testosterone was already staging a comeback.

A SHOT OF COURAGE?

Where sensitive straight man Alda may have exaggerated the hormone's evils, a macho gay man named Andrew Sullivan similarly hyped its power for good. Sullivan had injected testosterone into his own veins and then described the experience in a 2000 *New York Times Magazine* article titled "The He Hormone." Sullivan was using testosterone to counteract some of the effects of long-term HIV infection. "Within hours, and at most a day," he wrote, "I feel a deep surge of energy. It is less edgy than a double espresso, but just as powerful. My attention span shortens. In the two or three days after my shot, I find it harder to concentrate on my writing and feel the need to exercise more. My wit is quicker, my mind faster, but my judgment is more impulsive."

He's entitled to his own experience. It wasn't until later in the article that I started to squirm. "What our increasing knowledge of testosterone suggests is a core understanding of what it is to be a man, for better or worse. It is about the ability to risk for good and bad, to act, to strut, to dare, to seize."

As a woman, I'm left wondering whether the gutsy members of our sex are unfeminine, or even masculine. What about Amelia Earhart and Christiane Amanpour? What about female Navy and Air Force pilots and female astronauts? I can't help thinking that a woman should be entitled to act on an adventurous spirit without being accused of aping men. I, too, sometimes like to risk, to act, to strut, to dare, and to seize. Isn't that what makes life for either sex worth living?

Scientists often dismiss any single anecdotes as "a sample of one," not worthy of extending to more general conclusions. When I mentioned Andrew Sullivan's claims, biologists warned that it's impossible to detangle the placebo effect from any real influence testosterone was having on his mind. There have been some controlled studies on testosterone and sex differences, and those find, in general, much overlap between the sexes. The average man is taller, for example, than the average woman, but some women are taller than some men. Most personality and cognitive tests overlap significantly more than do measurements of height.

While it might be true that men make more testosterone than women, and it might also be true that higher-testosterone people take more risks, it's also likely that other factors influence risk-taking, energy, and action. Those other factors might endow some women with daring without rendering them masculine and give some men prudence without making them feminine.

Another testosterone-related trait that differs but overlaps between the sexes is spatial reasoning. I learned perhaps more than I wanted to about this while researching a column on a dating service that required a personality test. In taking it myself, I found some of the questions resembled a sort of intelligence test. In one, you had to determine the relative lengths of the horizontal and vertical pieces of a cross. In another you had to judge the relative sizes of two hexagons set against different backgrounds. The results came back immediately. I got them right, and was relieved, but only until I found out what those tests are supposed to mean.

One of the designers of the test was Rutgers University anthropologist Helen Fisher, best known for her books on mating, such as *The Anatomy of Love*. I called to ask her about these odd questions that seemed to have nothing to do with dating. "That measures testosterone," she said, and admitted she never gets those items right, being the feminine woman that she is. This was not what I was hoping to hear.

Can a couple of tests of spatial reasoning really indicate that I've got more than a ladylike allotment of testosterone? I asked Alan Booth, a Penn State University professor of sociology who's studied the effects of the male hormone. Booth said that the ability to judge spatial relationships does tend to reflect testosterone levels. "Males and females have had different roles for ten thousand years or more," he said. "Males needed to go on a big hunt. . . . They needed spatial abilities that are very acute, for aiming an ax or a stone." Women, he said, needed to be nurturing and good at relationships.

Ah, yes, but he apparently hasn't consulted the archaeologists and anthropologists we'll meet in later chapters. They're making the case that prehistoric men were out looking for dead things to scrape up as often as they were hunting, while women were making humanity's global expansion possible by sewing those clothes. Wouldn't you need spatial ability to thread needles?

For a while it was trendy to make a big deal of sex differences. Then, in the 1980s and nineties, similarity became all the rage. The pendulum has swung back in this century with another emphasis on the differences. It's easy to look at the sexes either way, since you can always find differences between the average man and the average woman, and yet many of us aren't average, so you can just as easily find women who are taller, more daring, better at spatial skills, more mechanical, and more mathematical than the average man. You can't accurately predict any of those traits in an individual by simply looking at whether there's a Y chromosome in someone's genes, or a penis in someone's jeans.

NO LONGER POISON

What's telling about Sullivan's story is that it argues so-called masculine behavior isn't hardwired but depends on your allotment of a hormone. And there are ways of changing your testosterone levels without giving yourself injections. Testosterone naturally continues to ebb and flow through life—even within the course of a day.

For women, testosterone is secreted by our adrenal glands, while for men it comes from the adrenals and the testes. The latest research shows it's crucial to female sex drive, and since it tends to decrease after menopause, older women are starting to experiment with testosterone patches to restore flagging libido. For men, too, aging depletes testosterone. But, oddly, getting married also causes male testosterone to drop by about 20 percent, while getting married and becoming a father can make it dip by 50 percent, said Peter Gray, an anthropologist at the University of Nevada. Scientists first saw this effect in groups of Army and Air Force veterans. Later Gray published a study that found the same effect in Chinese men.

Competition in sports or other arenas can sometimes make testosterone surge, said Penn State's Booth. A few years back he and colleagues studied male and female rugby players and found for both sexes testosterone levels rose before an event, and sports gave women a bigger hormone boost than it did men. Higher isn't necessarily better, said Booth. According to another study he and a colleague published in 1993, relatively low-testosterone men make the best husbands—or least they have the happiest relationships, especially when paired with low-testosterone women.

Conversely, newer studies are starting to dispute the old association between testosterone and ill health. "Conventional wisdom is that women live longer because estrogen is good and testosterone is bad," wrote Elizabeth Barrett-Connor, a professor of epidemiology at the University of California, San Diego, School of Medicine. She found something quite different after tracking testosterone and health in a group of nearly 800 men between the ages of fifty and ninety-one.

These men had been followed by doctors since the 1970s as part of a larger health survey, and what the data seemed to show was that the ones with the lowest testosterone were the most likely to die from heart disease and diabetes. But cause and effect can get hopelessly tangled in a study like this. Barrett-Connor also noticed that the lower-testosterone men were fatter around the middle. So it's possible that having low testosterone makes you fat and being fat can make you sick, though it's also possible that getting fat lowers your testosterone. Other researchers are finding that men's testosterone naturally decreases with age, but if it plunges too fast, it causes men to lose interest in their wives and often become depressed, which, in turn, can lead to other health troubles.

For women, too, it's hard to figure out whether testosterone is dictating our lives or our lives are dictating our testosterone levels. The implications are huge, considering that one study showed that women with high testosterone were slightly less likely to get married or have children. Does having a high testosterone level make you want to stay single, or do the cut-throat demands of sports and the job market spur some of us to make more male hormone? Perhaps Gloria Steinem was on to a biological truth when she noted that "some of us are becoming the men we always wanted to marry."

While the testosterone coursing through your veins right now might influence your sex drive, your health, and your mood, even more important may be the testosterone floating around when you were in the womb. It's then that our bodies are shaped into little boys or little girls and, as scientists now argue, sex hormones are also sculpting our developing brains.

The power of prenatal hormones may explain why closely related animals can vary so much in their behavior. Caring and monogamous male monkeys and penguins get a relatively low dose of testosterone, closer to their female counterparts, while showy peacocks or badass male gorillas get exposed to much more. In spotted hyenas, the female fetuses get a massive dose, which makes them dominant and territorial and gives them enlarged clitorises that they display the way other male mammals display their penises.

Sometimes within the same species and the same sex, testosterone can take an animal down one of several paths. In her book *Evolution's Rainbow*, Stanford University biologist Joan Roughgarden describes the case of white-throated sparrows, in which both females and males evolved two distinct types, separated by testosterone. Higher-testosterone males sport a white stripe and a penchant for aggressive, territorial behavior. Lower-testosterone males develop a tan stripe and are less territorial and better at protecting eggs and caring for babies. They can't switch between the two types. Surprisingly, the tan "feminine" males are more popular with the females, which also come in two types—a more aggressive white-marked female and a more laid-back tan one.

Humans have no telltale stripe to reveal whether we were high- or low-testosterone fetuses. Some scientists claim we do have a marker that is, thankfully, subtle. It's reflected in the relative length of your ring finger compared to your index finger. The average man has an index finger that's about 96 percent as long as his ring finger, while the average woman's index and ring fingers are almost exactly the same length. I learned all about fingers and sex at the 2006 meeting of the Human Behavior and Evolution Society, which brought about 500 researchers to the city of Philadelphia.

In a series of talks on that topic, researchers reassured audience members that many normal, healthy men and women have finger-length ratios more characteristic of the opposite sex. Judith Dubas from Utrecht University in the Netherlands said her latest research showed that women with a more "masculine" digit ratio have fewer children. She cited earlier results showing that men with a more "feminine" digit ratio were more prone to low sperm counts.

At that point those of us in the audience start nervously eyeing our hands. I thought my ring and index fingers looked about the same length, but it seemed to depend on how I held my hand. I found myself trying to angle it so that my index finger would look as long—and feminine—as possible. But since most people have a ratio of nearly one-to-one, the scientists say, you need high-precision calipers to get a real measurement.

In theory, the same prenatal testosterone that shapes our hands to some extent also shapes the relative masculinization of our brains. How is a masculine brain different from a feminine one? Catherine Salmon, a psychologist at Redlands University in California, decided to look for a connection between finger lengths and taste in erotica. It's been scientifically documented that many heterosexual men enjoy pornography depicting woman-on-woman sex. Women are on average not so keen on boy-boy porn, but Salmon told her audience at the meeting that a few women do enjoy stories featuring male homosexual encounters.

Such guy-on-guy erotica, I learned, often goes under the name of "slash fiction," not because there's any violence but to indicate a slash between the names of the lovers. It's part of a larger genre of "fanzine" literature in which fans of a movie or television show write their own stories about the characters. Slash started in the 1970s with that sexy *Star Trek* duo Kirk/Spock. A quick Web search reveals dozens of stories with passages like this shower scene: "Jim ran his free hand through Spock's wet, matted chest hair, rubbing the bronze-green nipples with his fingertips. . . . Spock moaned." The action gets much steamier at that point, and the pair eventually end up in a mind meld.

Many women find this unappealing to the point of disgust, Salmon said, but others report that it fulfills a long-held desire. She wondered whether the difference could be related to testosterone and perhaps connected to those finger-length ratios. To investigate, she lined up forty slash fans and thirty nonfans and measured their fingers with a pair of digital calipers. She found the controls averaged a very feminine index-to-ring ratio of 1.04. Fans measured, on average, 0.97, which is closer to the typical male ratio.

While Salmon's analysis showed this difference was statistically significant, a solitary result like this would need to be backed up by a couple of independent studies before it's going to impress the scientific community. As for me, I didn't find the Kirk/Spock thing erotic *or* disgusting. I found it quite hilarious. So I guess I won't know where I fit in on the masculinity scale unless I get a pair of digital calipers, which I don't plan to do.

MIDDLESEX

Many different genes orchestrate the workings of testosterone, and when only one malfunctions, the results can be dramatic. The consequences of one such testosterone-related mutation were detailed in the 2002 novel *Middlesex*. In this fictional account of a real disorder, a young Greek-American girl growing up in Detroit starts becoming a man when she hits puberty. The teenager shoots up to near six feet tall, her voice cracks, her breasts stay flat, and when a mustache appears, her mother, still in denial, takes him/her to a beauty parlor for waxing.

Author Jeffrey Eugenides identified the genetic anomaly to blame for his protagonist's plight as 5-alpha-reductase deficiency, a real disorder that crops up most often in Turkey, the Dominican Republic, and New Guinea. In the Dominican Republic, people with 5-alpha-reductase deficiency are called *guevedoche*, which is sometimes translated as "penis at twelve" or "balls at twelve." The *guevedoche* often look like girls when they're born, but at puberty their genitalia start to change—the clitoris growing until it looks more like a penis.

This is one of several things that can go awry in the pathway to human maleness. Even if you have a Y chromosome and as a fetus your incipient testes make testosterone, and you have all the right proteins to transport and respond to testosterone, some of it must be converted to a related compound called dihydrotestosterone in order to form the penis. That conversion depends on the critical enzyme 5-alpha-reductase, so if you can't make this enzyme, you don't get a normal penis. Instead, you may get what looks like a larger-than-average clitoris. Generally what the doctor sees when you're born would elicit a proclamation of "It's a girl."

Inside such little "girls" are usually undescended testicles, secreting testosterone. When someone with 5-alpha-reductase deficiency gets the usual surge of testosterone at puberty, that ambiguous organ starts to grow into something that looks more like a penis. Puberty also brings along a male body—muscular and without curves. In *Middlesex*, the main character, Callie, eventually changed her name to Cal, but in the end never felt or looked fully male.

In the late 1970s, Julianne Imperato-McGinley, an endocrinologist at Cornell Medical College, studied *guevedoche* in the Dominican Republic and found that of a sample of eighteen, all were reared as girls. Seventeen identified as males after they grew up, and of those, most started having sex with girls when they reached their teenage years. Just one continued to identify herself as female and went on to marry a man.

Years of debate followed the study. Imperato-McGinley took her study to indicate that the key to male identity is hormonal. It was the flood of testosterone at puberty, she reported, that made most of the *guevedoche* no longer "feel like girls" and later to feel like men. Other scientists paid more attention to the exceptions— the one who continued to live as a woman and another who considered himself to be a man but continued to dress in female clothing. Anthropologist Gilbert Herdt of San Francisco State University used these cases to bolster an argument for the power of culture to shape male or female identity.

The notion that gender follows culture more than biology was popular in the 1960s and early seventies. Johns Hopkins University sex researcher John Money led the charge. Money was so convinced of this mind-over-matter concept that he thought a boy lacking a normal penis could be raised as a girl. She'd be fine, he argued, with a little help from artificial estrogen and surgery. Money got the chance to test his idea in 1963 when a baby boy had his penis severely injured in a botched circumcision. Money advised the parents to let surgeons alter his genitalia to look female and then have him injected with female hormones so he could be raised as a girl. As journalist John Colapinto told the story in his book *As Nature Made Him*, things didn't turn out the way Money anticipated.

The little boy never wanted to be a girl, hated dresses and dolls, and loved tree-climbing and trucks. When he discovered what had happened to him, he started living as a man and got married, but later committed suicide. As scientists now understand, his brain had been shaped by male hormones while he was developing, so he was wired to see himself as a male.

THE MAKING OF A MAN

In transsexuals, however, that "wiring" may not go as expected. Like the boy in Money's misguided experiment, Max Wolf Valerio also saw himself as a boy from the start, though in his case he was born unambiguously as a girl. I interviewed him in 2005, when he was forty-nine, having lived as a man for the last seventeen years. Like many female-to-male transsexuals, he could pass as an ordinary guy. When I told my colleagues I was writing about a woman who became a man, they all asked the same questions: Did doctors attach a penis? Does it work? I'll get to that, but, as Valerio discovered, the essence of maleness is not nearly as phallocentric as Freud would have us believe.

From his perspective as a person who's seen life from both sides, Valerio considers masculinity to be hormonal. Testosterone alone was enough to take him most of the way through his one-way journey to manhood, which he chronicled in his 2006 book *The Testosterone Files*. Born as a girl named Anita, she insisted for some time that she was a boy, and only reluctantly accepted being a very tomboyish girl. She grew into a tall and exotic redhead—part Hispanic, part Blackfoot Indian—who favored black hair dye and motorcycle jackets. Now, as Max, he said no one thinks he's anything but a guy. When he goes to transsexual support meetings, people either don't know why he's there or assume he's trying to become a woman. He wrote the book, he said, to offer his perspective on the nature of masculinity and femininity, culture and biology, and the war between the sexes.

Valerio, who lives in San Francisco, had always been attracted exclusively to women. But during her years as Anita she came to realize she was different from other lesbians. "I thought all lesbians really wanted to be men," Valerio said. She didn't like to be touched sexually because in order to enjoy such activity, she needed to fantasize that she was a man. And, unlike her lesbian friends, she was turned on by traditionally feminine women who wore high heels, makeup, and short skirts.

Still, friends thought she was crazy to consider a sex change. Few people had heard of female-to-male transsexuals in the early 1980s. She was a strikingly good-looking woman, they told her. "Why risk ending up looking like Julie Andrews in a fake mustache?"

But at thirty-two, she started injecting testosterone directly into her thigh. During the next few months, her jawline and waist filled out, a beard grew, and her muscles hardened and bulked up. She developed a ravenous appetite and her voice changed to a perfectly natural male one. Living as a man, he eventually had his breasts removed. Seventeen years later, at forty-nine, he'd still not had any surgery on his genitals. The hormones enlarged his clitoris so much that it grew to the size of his thumb when erect. He said it looks much like a penis now and he uses it to have intercourse with his girlfriend.

This is not as unusual as it sounds, said Marci Bowers, a Colorado surgeon and expert on sex change. Testosterone does make the clitoris grow, and using it for sex this way is "increasingly typical" for newly male transsexuals. A few opt for surgery that constructs a penis from a tissue graft, she said, but it's an expensive procedure. Others have a simpler operation called a metoidioplasty, which extends the clitoris and makes it more penis-like.

But for Valerio, the real surprise was the way testosterone transformed his mind. "If I looked at an object, it seemed more defined, more three-dimensional," he said. Words came with more effort, and emotions became harder to articulate. His sex drive soared. When Valerio was still Anita, she and her lesbian friends thought men's leering, lustful behavior was nothing but posturing. He changed his attitude toward men once he became one and felt male lust firsthand.

Some scientists studying sex differences have turned to transsexuals for insights. Neuroscientists Ruben and Raquel Gur of the University of Pennsylvania worked with a female-to-male transsexual, also named Max, and found that as the testosterone shots kicked in, he improved on spatial-skills tests, like the one I took on the dating quiz. And he got worse at verbal fluency. It's just an anecdotal, preliminary investigation, but along with a few similar observations it hints at our inborn differences. Valerio's transformation also points to where we are the same—in our creative drives, intellectual curiosity, and humanity. Despite all the changes wrought by testosterone, he said, "I'm still basically the same person."

8. THE SECRET LIVES OF SPERM

WHAT SPERM WANT AND HOW THEY CAN MANIPULATE BOTH MEN AND WOMEN

One of the more degrading expressions men use to describe one another's less-than-monogamous behavior is "thinking with the little head," and I couldn't help wondering if there was a deeper truth embedded in this slight. Biologist Richard Dawkins argued in his book *The Selfish Gene* that we all evolved, in part, to serve the reproductive needs of our genes. That's why many of us seek out status, fuss over our looks, and form relationships with certain types of partners, even at the cost of our own happiness and/or sanity. Of course most genes are embedded in our cells and die with us. Only the copies of your genes lucky enough to find themselves in your eggs or sperm have a hope for long-term survival. Perhaps the whole pickup school/game/seduction phenomenon is being driven by the needs of selfish sperm, and men might say they're thinking with the little head when they're really thinking with millions of *microscopic* heads.

Men and their sperm evolved jointly as teammates, each adapting to advance the interests of the other. And there's more to sperm than meets even the microscope-aided eye. "Sperm are just so central to so many aspects of biology," said Scott Pitnick, a biologist at Syracuse University who studies sperm evolution, among other things. They're like part of you and yet they're like free-living organisms, he said. "And we send them away from our bodies into foreign environments." In some animals, such as turtles, sperm can live for years inside the female. Human sperm just get about seventy-two hours.

Though all male animals are defined as male by their sperm, not all sperm look spermlike, Pitnick said. "Sperm are the most diverse cells there are. . . . Nothing else comes close to sperm." There are tailless sperm that ooze along like amoebas, spiny sperm, and sperm that come out decorated with all sorts of weird extensions—even grappling hooks. Because they vary so widely, even among very similar animals, many biologists use sperm to help them sort out evolutionary relationships. Sperm matter when it comes to understanding the formation of new species and for tracking biodiversity.

Sperm evolve to compete with other sperm and to contend with whatever they encounter in the female reproductive tract. Sometimes females evolve tricks to eject unwanted sperm or to favor some sperm over others. "Clearly the females are controlling the game," said Pitnick. Sperm subsequently coevolve to adapt to this, as do the males ejaculating them.

EVERY SPERM IS SACRED

Cultural attitudes toward sex also evolved in tandem with the scientific understanding of sperm. Nobody knew anything about sperm until the 1600s. The first person to report seeing them was Antoni van Leeuwenhoek, who happened to be the first person to reconfigure the new invention known as the microscope so it could resolve objects that small. After examining pond water and discovering microbes, he filled a slide with his own semen and discovered sperm. Perhaps to avoid any prurient speculation, the Dutch microscopist included in his report the disclaimer that the sperm were obtained "upon the excess with which Nature provided me in my conjugal relations."

At first, the world being rather sexist, people thought sperm contained the entire makings for a new person. Little people actually existed inside sperm, they thought, and some scientists claimed to have seen them. You might think such a theory unfair and belittling to women, who go through so much trouble and pain to deliver children, but the sperm-are-babies theory would come back to bite the male sex. Embedded in sperm, those "preformed" people faced many hazards, and the sexual mores of the eighteenth and nineteenth centuries were aimed in part to protect them, said Lee Silver, a biologist at Princeton University and author of the 2006 book *Challenging Nature*. "It was illegitimate for men to ejaculate through masturbation or to engage in oral or anal sex," said Silver, any of which activities would send the preformed humans to an unseemly end.

Before sperm were discovered, people still connected semen

with the "seed" that started a pregnancy, and so the evils of masturbation had long been established in Western culture. In the early fifth century A.D., Augustine rated it as a crime worse than rape, incest, or adultery, since it was nonreproductive and hence "unnatural." In the thirteenth century, Thomas Aquinas seconded the taboo. Later, many religious leaders confused the biblical story of Onan (Genesis 38:9) with masturbation, though most scholars say it's really about birth control through coitus interruptus.

In the 1700s, masturbation was considered not only harmful to the sperm but to the man himself. The writings of influential Swiss physician Samuel-Auguste Tissot established a persistent belief that semen was such a precious fluid that one ounce was equivalent to forty ounces of blood. Masturbation, Tissot warned, could lead to epilepsy, memory loss, weakened backs, acne, gonorrhea, and syphilis, among other horrible maladies. It was an attitude satirized by the film *Dr. Strangelove,* in which the character General Jack D. Ripper worried that sex would drain away his "essence."

Any illusion that our own puritanical Western society victimizes only women is quickly dispelled in reading about all the ways boys were prevented from masturbating in the 1800s. Some were confined in straitjackets or wrapped in cold, wet sheets while sleeping. Doctors applied leeches to boys' penises to remove blood, or "congestion"; male genitals were burned with electric currents, hot irons, and caustic chemicals. Or a boy's penis was stuck in a metal "cage" that sounded an alarm if he had an erection.

Many of these treatments were applied to girls, too, and a few got surgery to remove the clitoris. According to some sources, preventing masturbation was the main impetus behind the standard American medical practice of circumcising boys from the nineteenth century to today. Doctors continued to believe in the dangers of masturbation well into the twentieth century, and solo sex wasn't pronounced safe by the American Medical Association until 1972.

We now understand that sperm carry just half the genetic code for making a baby. Still, they are amazing entities in themselves. When you're fifty micrometers long and blind, the task of navigating four to five inches of the female reproductive tract must rival crossing the straits of Magellan. Only a few succeed while the vast majority die trying. It now appears that sperm carry chemical and thermal sensory equipment and can swim with different strokes depending on whether they're gliding up the uterus or breaking down the thick zona pellucida that surrounds and protects the ultimate goal, the egg. Sperm don't just thrash around randomly, said Yuriy Kirichok, a biologist at Harvard University. They home in on their targets like heat-seeking missiles, swimming from colder places to warmer. Even more surprising, he said, was the discovery that sperm may be able to smell. We humans have more than 1,000 different molecular smell sensors, known as olfactory receptors. Most of them are expressed in the nose, but a few crop up in sperm. In experiments, Kirichok found that sperm will swim toward increasing concentrations of a synthetic compound called bourgeonal, the scent of which he characterizes as "floral."

While some sperm are lone explorers, others work in teams. British scientists announced in 2007 that they'd found rats and mice both make sperm with hooks that help them cooperate with each other, several hundred of them linking up in chains once they get into the female. That way they can swim faster and beat sperm from other males to an egg.

At England's University of Bath, biologists Timothy Karr and Steve Dorus found that sperm carry 341 different types of complex molecules, or proteins. Proteins are more than mere passive substances—they make up the active molecular-scale machinery that runs our bodies. The 2006 finding was hailed by other scientists as the most complete protein catalogue, or proteome, yet recorded for an animal cell. Karr said he did not follow the Dutch tradition of van Leeuwenhoek and use his own sperm, but instead extracted them from an experimental animal—a species of fruit fly known as drosophila. This might sound harder than getting sperm from a human, and it's clearly not good for the fly. It involves dissection tools and, sadly, Karr explained, the fly doesn't survive.

One of the most striking differences between human sperm and drosophila sperm is that the fly sperm are, improbably, a hundred times longer than ours. In fact, the tail stretches as long as the fly itself, equivalent to a man producing a six-foot sperm. You might think the male fly would almost have to give birth to his sperm, but the skinny tail can ball up like a strand of thread that fits easily inside the fly. (The world-record longest sperm measures more than two inches and comes from a different species of fruit fly.)

Once he had extracted and ground up some fly sperm, Karr put them through a mass spectrometer, which separates the sperm's component molecules according to their masses. The proteins pick up an electric charge and the machine sends them flying through an electric field, the lighter ones following a different trajectory from the heavier ones.

While men produce less extravagant sperm than do fruit flies, they make them in vast quantities—about 300 million for every ejaculation. To some, that might seem like 299,999,999 sperm too many, but that's how men manage to compete with other men, said zoologist Robin Baker, who talked to me on the phone from

Spain, where he moved after retiring from the University of Manchester. Baker was determined to overturn the conventional wisdom that the male body was inefficient and wasteful when it comes to sperm. It's really women's fault, he said. Men have to make lots of sperm partly because over the many thousands of years of evolutionary time, women did, in fact, sometimes fool around.

Thanks to evolutionary pressure induced by runaround women, men don't just shoot out millions of sperm at random. There's a surprising amount of control and nuance. Baker speculated in his 1996 book *Sperm Wars* that sperm come in different varieties, some for fertilizing the egg, some for blocking other sperm, and some "killers" that commit selective spermicide against rivals. Baker also proposed that men can unconsciously adjust the number of sperm released depending on the intended destination. If they are headed into a woman's vagina, a man will subconsciously assess the likely competition and adjust accordingly. Baker also argues that masturbation has a reproductive function—it helps a man eject old, feeble sperm, which are quickly replaced by freshly minted ones. In this view, male masturbation could be seen as a form of housecleaning. To test these ideas, Baker, working with Mark Bellis, asked male volunteers to use condoms to collect samples, and found, among other things, that the longer a man's partner had been away since the last time he had sex with her, the higher his sperm count the next time. The pattern held even when men admitted to cleaning out a few old sperm in the interim.

Some of Baker's ideas were met with skepticism by the wider scientific community, but Florida Atlantic University evolutionary psychologist Todd Shackelford has picked up where Baker left off. He found that on average, if a man's partner had gone out of town since the last time he had sex, he would see her as more sexually attractive and would want to have sex with her more when she returned. The longer they were out of sight of each other, the greater the increased desire. The effect was independent of how long ago they'd last had sex.

Men's desires, both conscious and unconscious, evolved to help sperm do their jobs. And sperm evolved to advance the reproductive agendas of men. Both are steered by the evolution of women and the agendas of our eggs. The sexes and the sex cells are all intertwined.

9. ARE MEN SCUM?

PORNOGRAPHY AND CASUAL SEX
IN PERSPECTIVE

Men may have their own anatomy and physiology but can they also claim a distinctively male brain? If so, is there anything male brains do that their female counterparts don't?

How male and female brains differ has become a politically explosive question—one that cost a former Harvard president his position and perhaps his reputation. It's still politically correct and relatively safe to talk about differences as long as the males are being denigrated. That's been the case for some years. Back in the 1990s, David Buss, a professor of evolutionary psychology, was trying to explain some experimental results about sex differences to one of his classes at the University of Texas. In anonymous surveys, women said they didn't desire one-night stands. Men said they did. Women responded that they wanted about one sex partner in the next two years and four or five in a lifetime. Men wanted two within the month, eight in the next two years, and eighteen over a lifetime.

The differences got even more striking when asked how long

they'd need to know someone before engaging in sex. Women wanted about a year before they'd be willing to commit a definite "yes." Men admitted they'd probably have sex with a woman they'd known for a week. Buss started to explain the findings in terms of evolutionary psychology when one young woman raised her hand to say, "Professor Buss, I have a simpler explanation for your data—men are slime."

Harvard evolutionary psychologist and linguist Steven Pinker relates the above anecdote in his book *How the Mind Works*. He then poses the question: Are men really slime or are they just trying to look like slime? His conclusion: they're really slime. Chalk it up to age and experience, perhaps, but I didn't see things the same way as Buss's student. I was impressed that the average man surveyed only wanted eighteen women. The men taking pickup artist boot camp surely aspired to more than this—and some had already surpassed it.

None of that seemed particularly slimy. Harder to understand, however, is the way males tend to condemn women for wanting a little sexual variety. Many men as a matter of course expect more self-restraint from women than they would consider practicing themselves. Ron Geraci, author of a dating tell-all called *The Bachelor Chronicles,* lays it all out unabashedly in a chapter titled "Humble Pleas From a Single American Male": "Do not sleep with me unless we've had four dates. If you have no interest in dating me seriously and don't see any chance of us having a relationship, use me like the dirty whore that I am. . . . Make coffee, please, too." When I confronted Geraci, then thirty-six, he admitted he doesn't quite understand why he feels this way. "Maybe I have Groucho Marx syndrome," he said, referring to Groucho's famous statement that he wouldn't want to belong to any club that would have him as a member. A native of southern New Jersey, Geraci found himself thrust into the role of dating columnist while working as an editor for *Men's Health*. He wrote of his own adventures and misadventures—from the alluring tease who got away to the former lesbian who slept with him and then baked him cookies. Single men, he said, have sex for the same reason animals eat when they see food. It's the "you never know where your next meal is coming from" instinct, which may also explain male behavior around buffet tables and beer kegs.

In person, Geraci looks just as he describes himself in print. He's about five-foot-six and a little plump (but in a cute way), with a mischievous smile. For our interview he picked out a quiet neighborhood saloon near his Greenwich Village apartment. "I wanted people to know what was in men's heads," he said. Some of it may seem superficial, "but often a man's motives are noble." He says he's desperate to play the role of husband and provider, just not with any of the women who have agreed to have sex with him before four dates. "I want a woman to be discriminating," he said. If she sleeps with you right away, it's a sign you could probably do better.

Where does this attitude come from? Are men really doomed by evolution to uphold this double standard or is it just the baggage imposed by Western patriarchal culture? I turned to Dr. Buss, the University of Texas professor whose lecture prompted the female student's "men are slime" theory. "It's definitely an evolved sex difference," he said. Human males and females are saddled with two major sources of inequality, he explained. First of all, for most of human existence there was no DNA testing, which meant men didn't have the luxury of knowing for sure that the children they were feeding were really their genetic offspring. Avoiding cuckolding is a big driving force in male behavior across nature.

Buss and other evolutionary psychologists argue that preference for relatively chaste women evolved to help men avoid the evolutionary trap of raising someone else's offspring. Women didn't evolve the same distaste for men who've slept around, and if anything, said Buss, it piques women's interest in a guy when we discover other women wanted him. Which is why Geraci can get away with admitting to the world that he's had more than a few one-night stands without hampering his quest for a mother of his future children.

In his own wide-ranging surveys, Buss said, he found this double standard holds across cultures, though American men care about female chastity more than men in Sweden, Norway, Finland, and a few other Northern European countries. But, thankfully, our men are not quite as purity-obsessed as the men in Iran or China. In those same studies Buss also found that men worldwide had relatively low standards when it came to casual sex. They were willing to forgo education, charm, honesty, independence, kindness, intelligence, and emotional stability. The only qualities that turned men off for short-term mating were low sex drive, physical unattractiveness, need for commitment, and hairiness.

Of course, a minority of men like hairiness.

AGE CANNOT WITHER HER

And some men like older women, but most, unfortunately, prefer them young. If there was ever a case for men being slime, it would be the writer of this e-mail, sent after I wrote a column on sex and aging:

"Frankly, I don't want to think about gnarly, fat, flabby, wrinkled, jowly, grayhaired old hags having sex with ANYBODY. Stop trying to fight nature! I resent your categorization of the normal older man/younger woman relationship as dirty. IT is totally natural and normal for a man of any age to be attracted to a young woman. IF God wanted old hags to have sex he wouldn't have invented menopause!!! Men of ANY/EVERY age will always prefer young, nubile women to erection-killing hags any day, if they can get them. A fresh young girl makes a man happy to be alive. The only men who will have sex with old hags are either gay or gigolos. GET USED TO IT!!! Even a hot 50 year old must hit the wall at some point. Most women your age can't handle the truth. It's the Terry McMillan syndrome. Thank God that there are plenty of sweet young babes who can be swayed by money/looks/fame/power. Unfortunately, I don't have any of them and I am only in my late 40's but I would rather be alone than have to settle for a old cougar. Grannies should take care of their grandchildren and leave sex to the young."

This, thank God, represents an extreme case, and there are some outliers on the other side as well. The same article prompted a call from a thirty-three-year-old male reader named Jesse who wanted me to investigate his curious attraction to older women—much older—in their seventies and eighties. Varicose veins turn him on, he said, and he's a big fan of "granny porn," which features explicit images of older women.

What's interesting about this geriatric fetish, known as gerontophilia, is not that it happens but that it's considered so extraordinary. Most men's attitudes are closer to the bitter, ageist guy who e-mailed me his nasty missive. Because the vast majority of men seek out or even worship youth, we women invest in all sorts of products to appear young—skin creams, hair dyes, and, more recently, Botox. We women all know what Joan Collins meant when she quipped that the problem with beauty is that it's like being born rich and getting poorer.

And what makes it all the more painful is that this youth premium doesn't apply to many other creatures. Scientists recently found, for example, that chimpanzee females grow sexier with age. Chimp males are natural gerontophiles. Boston University anthropologist Martin Muller and colleagues observed this pattern over many years of following wild chimpanzees at Kibale National Park in Uganda. Muller's team found that males in the troop tend to ignore the chimp equivalent of nubile teenage girls. Even more surprising, females get increasingly more male attention as they age. Grandmother chimps are considered the hottest and are fought over the most.

We human beings find that odd, perhaps, because of a biological quirk known as menopause. The females of most other species, including chimpanzees, remain fertile for more than 90 percent of their lives, said Bobbi Low, an evolutionary biologist at the University of Michigan. For female diamondback terrapins, that can mean more than a century of sex and fecundity. When a twenty-year-old male meets a hundred-year-old female, he mates with the same enthusiasm he'd show a turtle his own age. In our menopausal species, however, men with a taste for older women are less likely to procreate, so any genetic tendency to prefer older women tends to die out, thus breeding into the human race a preference for nubile girls.

You can also blame men's youth fetish on monogamy, said evolutionary psychologist Buss, whom we met earlier in this chapter. It's not that all humans are monogamous, but many do mate for years, and some for life. A male is likely to produce more children if he picks a wife of nineteen than one of forty-five. As a long-term mate, he said, a woman in her late teens offers the highest "reproductive potential." Argue all you want about inner beauty and the value of experience, but studies across cultures find female allure is nearly always tied to youth, if not synonymous with it.

Chimp females don't have to deal with menopause or monogamy. The females are not just promiscuous, they're almost frantically so. "It looks like their primary goal is to mate with all the males," Muller said. In fact, they can mate with as many as fifty males in one day. This behavior probably evolved, he said, to protect their young. Males of many species tend to kill their rivals' babies—but not their own—before mating. In light of that threat, those females that slept around the most and thus gave more of the local males a shot at being father ended up with the most surviving offspring. Anything less than total sluttishness could be deemed juvenile-endangerment.

Harder to explain is why male chimps find the oldest females even hotter than the merely middle-aged. Both are equally fertile and both have the experience necessary to protect their offspring. Muller offered one possible explanation: chimp females climb the dominance ranks with age, giving them and their babies better access to territory and food.

Luckily for our older women, humans are a varied species with many individuals who break the rules, such as the forty-something who married actress Gina Lollobrigida after she turned eighty. A gerontophile? The tabloids say they've been together for years. Maybe he just loved her.

Another behavior that might feed the "men are slime" theory is the consumption of pornography. The first time I wrote about pornography for my newspaper column, I discovered it's a touchy subject. Women complained that, by saying men buy more porn, I was implying that porn-loving women are "freaks." That makes about as much sense as calling tall women freaks because most women are shorter than most men. It's just that women are much less likely than men to consider viewing porn a valuable use of their time or money. Some of us are just more drawn to shoes.com than sex.com.

In his book *Sexual Investigations*, philosopher of sex Alan Soble explains it this way: "Men are sometimes horny for the touch, the closeness of a woman; sometimes they are so hungry for a woman and her sex, they seek photos that help put to sleep their yearning desires," he wrote. "The whole world knows this and humiliates men, embarrasses them, makes them feel guilty."

I don't want to add to the humiliation, but it is curious that men like looking at pornographic images and movies. There's no obvious evolutionary payoff here. The people in these films are obviously busy. They're not inviting you in to join them.

British zoologist Robin Baker, now retired from the University of Manchester, told me that men love pornography more than women do thanks to an ancient adaptation inherited from other male animals. Many male mammals, he said, get aroused watching other animals (of their own species) doing it. In rats and monkeys, for example, if a male runs across a pair mating, he will not only become aroused at the sight but will move sperm into his urethra. Which means, as Baker puts it, "he's loaded and ready to fire."

In the evolutionary game, such a reaction could prove advantageous if a male is tough enough to force the other guy off and take over, or sneaky enough to wait till he leaves and then move in while the female is still in the mood. Humans tend to have sex in private, so such opportunities don't present themselves often, but the instinct could remain with us, to be exploited by pornographers.

When I posed the porn question to Harvard psychologist Pinker, he said that male birds will try to mate with anything resembling a female of the species—a stuffed female or even just the head of a stuffed female. "The sight of a fertile member of the opposite sex would normally correlate with an opportunity to make babies," he said. In Pinker's view, porn fools your body into reacting instinctively, as if the images were real. Pinker goes on to link men's taste for pornography to one of the most salient behavior differences between men and women: men get more excited by the prospect of sex with a total stranger. And, assuming you don't have many friends who are porn stars, porn provides images of strangers with whom you have not shared so much as a cup of coffee.

In their quest to better understand human sexuality, researchers sometimes collect volunteers and show them pornographic images or films under controlled laboratory conditions. At McGill University in Montreal, for example, psychologist Irv Binik recently used such images to compare their effects on men and women.

To get beyond the self-reporting of the volunteers, which was bound to be colored by cultural taboos, he hooked them up to an instrument called a thermograph, which can sense remotely how much blood flows to the genital area. What he found was that men and women reacted with equal speed when watching pornographic films. Binik said he used special sex films borrowed from the Kinsey Institute in Indiana—one that had been determined to be arousing to men, the other to women. Binik said both films showed your standard heterosexual couplings (and both looked about the same to him, he said).

So what's going on with the women in this McGill study? Is there something funny about Canadians? Why don't women buy more porn if, as reported, we're just as aroused by it as men?

One explanation that sometimes gets casually offered up is that men are somehow "more visual than women." It's almost always uttered by men as an excuse for either looking at pornography or ogling women other than their partners. Is there any science behind this claim?

As it happens, Michael Platt of Duke University is studying sex differences in the way we respond to pictures. What he found: on average, men will pay to see images of women but you have to pay women to look at images of men. Platt, who is a neurobiologist and an anthropologist, started with studying sex differences in monkeys. Monkeys and apes respond to photographs much the way we humans do. The rhesus macaques that Platt studied seem to recognize faces of familiar monkeys.

He found that male macaques liked looking at female rear ends and faces of dominant males. They liked these enough to pay by sacrificing the chance to get a treat. But you had to bribe them with the same treats to get them to look at female macaque faces or the faces of subordinate males.

Female macaques develop pink swellings around their rear ends when they near ovulation, so male monkeys were probably programmed by natural selection to respond to this, said Platt. And males are similarly motivated to collect potentially lifesaving information by studying dominant males. He hadn't yet gotten access to female macaques to do the reverse study but he's moved on to study both male and female humans.

For them, he took images from a website called hotornot.com. Male subjects, on average, would pay a small amount of money (the human version of treats) or would work hard pressing buttons to see pictures of women from the site. But that didn't work in reverse. "For the most part, you had to pay females to look at any male pictures—even those where the guys were rated super hot," he said. This could help explain why the big market for internet pornography is male, and why men's magazines featuring scantily clad women continue to abound.

In the human experiments, the subjects were asked not just to look at pictures but to rate them. Male subjects enjoyed the task and many wanted to keep going even after an hour or so, said Platt. After about ten minutes of hotornot.com, women were begging to stop.

To probe further into the effects of sexual imagery on the human brain, a group of scientists at Emory University in Atlanta put men and women under a brain-scanning machine known as functional MRI and showed them erotic images. Men and women both reported being aroused by the pictures, which featured nude men, nude women, and opposite-sex couples engaged in sex acts. Both sexes showed activity in the visual cortex, but in comparing the responses of men and women, they found just one difference—in men the pictures caused more activation in a region known as the amygdala.

"Historically the amygdala has been seen as the center for fear and learning," said psychologist Kim Wallen, one of the authors of the Emory study. "More recently it appears the amygdala is involved in emotion." He speculated that men may find sexy pictures more emotionally salient than do women. They get more of an emotional charge from them.

The experiment can't determine whether it's ingrained in male nature to respond this way to pornography, or it's something acquired through the way boys and girls are socialized. It also doesn't make any moral judgment. Why should just looking at anything qualify a person as scum or slime?

But it's not just politically correct coeds who say men are, essentially, slime by nature. The same sentiment came with no prompting, for example, when I was interviewing Phillip Longman, a demographics expert and fellow at the think tank New America Foundation. Longman was telling me about patriarchy, using a variation on the "men are slime" theory to explain why men tend to periodically reject it. In his definition, patriarchy is more than male dominance. It requires both sexes to live highly choreographed lives. Men are not just pressured to marry but are also limited to women of the right religion, status, family line, etc. Once married, a man provides money and takes charge, and the woman bears as many babies as nature provides. It's not always good for him.

In a patriarchal society, children take the man's name. Money and property pass down exclusively through male lines. Men are taught to value "honor," which they achieve through the children who bear their name. Patriarchy isn't maintained by the desires of men but by its own fecundity, Longman said. Patriarchal societies produce more kids than egalitarian or matriarchal ones. And it's not surprising that people who believe an all-powerful deity wants them to "go forth and multiply" will do so faster than those who don't hold such a belief.

That's where the "men are slime" idea came up. Longman said men tend to reject patriarchy because it pressures them to get married, which goes against their Darwinian instincts "to have as many children as possible by as many women as possible." This alleged male sluttiness explains why patriarchy has waxed and waned over the centuries, despite the system's natural tendency to spread, said Longman. While children tend to hold on to a family's patriarchal values, they can sometimes defect, and occasionally do so in droves—as happened during the Roman Empire and in the 1960s in the United States. Both times, men and women started to value individual expression and happiness—and men got horny and hungry for variety.

It's not that I'm naïve enough to assume men have no desire for sex with various women, but I'm inclined to believe men also possess a genuine desire for connection and a capacity for long-term love. I found some men who agree. Some see male "slimy" behavior not as the opposite of patriarchy but as a product of it—the system's own bastard child. Calvin Sandborn, a fifty-seven-year-old former macho man, said that without patriarchy, men would sleep around less, not more. He explains his view in his 2007 memoir *Becoming the Kind Father.* The son of a drunken, violent father, Sandborn described his younger self as a steely, stoic provider. He worked long hours as an environmental lawyer in Victoria, Canada. He yelled at his kids, and eventually his anger precipitated the breakup of his twenty-five-year marriage.

After some soul-searching, he started seeing the shadow of patriarchy hanging over his sad, deflated life. It's a system that demands that men seize and maintain power, he said. But that denies men the ability to enjoy the true intimacy of an egalitarian relationship. And it denies them the ability to admit to vulnerability. "While women lose their voices under patriarchy, men lose their hearts," he said.

When I asked him about male promiscuity, he said that while some nineteen-year-olds want to sow the proverbial wild oats, most eventually grow past this. "I've known some very hardened men who talk about screwing everyone," he said, but he attributes this attitude to the male inability to feel, thanks to patriarchy's relentless pressure on men to appear powerful and dominant. Under patriarchy, he said, men become hardened through a system of hazing. A man who showed "feminine" emotional sensitivity was not a real man but was condemned as a "sissy," "wimp," "wuss," or "pussy." In his view, if you got rid of patriarchy you could free men to love their wives and children in a way that's impossible in a culture where every relationship is hierarchical.

When evolutionary psychologist David Buss surveyed men, after all, they didn't say they wanted to sleep with as many women as possible. They said they wanted only eighteen. When I called Buss, he reminded me that that figure was an average. Some want more, some want fewer. He's come to the conclusion that human males follow different strategies when it comes to finding love and sex. Some males just want to sleep around and some want to settle down, while others want a little of both. We're not as hardwired in our behavior as other animals, and so we may never disentangle our animal instincts from our culture. Therefore, if you define slime (or scum) by promiscuity, then some men are and some are not, and therefore the answer to the question "Are men scum?" is no.

Buss is not one to shy away from the ugly side of male nature. In his 2005 book *The Murderer Next Door* he describes a male instinct for sexual jealousy and connects it to the fact that men are much more likely than women to kill or injure their own spouses or partners. Some cultures breed more male jealousy-fueled violence than others, and in demographer Longman's view, patriarchal ones are the worst. A patriarchal society's obsession with honor and family can magnify a man's natural jealous tendencies.

To maintain the sexual fidelity of his wife and the purity of his daughters, a man may cloister them, or make them cover up in burkas. Even in the twenty-first century human-rights workers continue to report that in some Middle Eastern countries, families sometimes engage in "honor killings" of unfaithful wives or unmarried daughters suspected of having lost their virginity.

Though all this sounds terribly primitive, Longman is convinced that patriarchy is in ascendancy worldwide. That's because those who hold more egalitarian beliefs just aren't breeding fast enough to keep up. For doubters, Longman laid out his case in an article titled "The Return of Patriarchy" that ran in the March/April 2006 issue of *Foreign Policy* magazine and inspired the chilling cover teaser: "Why Men Rule and Conservatives Will Inherit the Earth."

Among the states that voted for President Bush in 2004, he wrote, fertility rates are 12 percent higher than in states that went for Kerry. Though liberal commentators often dismiss the religious right as a vocal minority, he said, American culture really is drifting toward fundamentalism. Not that it can keep drifting forever. The trend will almost certainly turn around again, as it did during the Roman Empire, the 1960s, and many periods in between. For complex reasons people will start to crave more sexual freedom and more egalitarian relationships. As it has declined before, patriarchy will decline again even if men aren't all slime.

10. BEAUTY AND BEASTS

HOW THE QUEST FOR SEX
GAVE RISE TO BEAUTY

was to look for a six-foot-five man wearing black nail polish.
That was my instruction from the publicist working with Mystery, the man who launched a whole industry of seduction seminars and boot camps. I'd seen his picture on the flap of his book
jacket. He held his hands so as to display the painted nails. His hair
was gathered in a long ponytail, his head covered with a fuzzy,
floppy hat. He looked like he'd painted his own stripe on the transgender rainbow.

A fashionable half-hour late, Mystery finally swept into the
room, followed by a small entourage. He looked a little like a
swashbuckling pirate, with his long suede coat that was cut to look
tattered at the hem, cowboy-type hat, pointy boots, and various
other accessories—a pair of opera glasses, an earring in each ear,
lip stud, and a heart-shaped locket around his neck. "Don't you
want to know what's in it?" he teased.

I knew from reading his book that Mystery was "peacocking"—
wearing clothing or other items that stand out and often beg some

sort of explanation. A man or woman with attention-getting garb is said to be heavily peacocked.

And why not? Peacocks seem to have it made, just strutting around and looking good while the females flutter after them. When it comes to nest building or taking care of offspring or other such drudgery, "the male doesn't do anything," said Adeline Loyau, a French biologist who studies these birds and their peculiar mating habits. But a peacock's life is not as easy as it appears.

When real peacocks engage in peacocking, biologists call it sexual ornamentation. The sapphire- and emerald-spotted tails are considered ornamental because they don't help the peacocks survive. Peahens have inconspicuous brown feathers that probably keep them better hidden from predators. Some scientists say we humans are loaded with such evolutionary flourishes—prominent breasts and buttocks decorating women, and muscles and facial hair adorning some men. In his book *The Mating Mind*, evolutionary psychologist Geoffrey Miller argues that human creative intelligence also evolved as a sort of sexual ornament.

Charles Darwin was the first to explain sexual ornamentation, after allegedly being flummoxed by peacocks strutting through English gardens. The birds even reportedly gave him bouts of nausea because he couldn't see how the striking but cumbersome tails would have evolved or why they only graced the male of the species. Darwin's problem with peacocks came at a point when he'd already formulated his theory of evolution by natural selection, which posited that changes in living things are driven by survival of the fittest, or, more accurately, by survival of the offspring of the fittest. Natural selection explained how so many plants and animals acquired exquisite adaptations to their environments—from the white coat of the polar bear to the water-thrifty ways of the desert tortoise.

But if anything, peacock tails appeared to saddle the males with a survival handicap, attracting predators and weighing the males down. Eventually Darwin solved the riddle, realizing that the peahens in a sense designed the tails through their sexual predilections. As long as the peahens kept mating only with males sporting the largest or most colorful tails, each generation would produce ever larger or more colorful ones. Like farmers trying to get better chickens or cattle, the peahens were breeding traits into their own males. Darwin called this process sexual selection. It was this other part of evolution that he described in his second great book, *The Descent of Man, and Selection in Relation to Sex.*

For being graced with such extreme ornaments, peacocks can blame (or thank) the sexual habits of the peahens. Instead of each peahen choosing her own sexual partner, they all flock to the same few males. "It's like Beatlemania," Miller said. The peahens would rather wait their turn for the popular males than accept any number of more mediocre-looking males that would be happy to mate with them. By acting like groupies, females can up the ante for male beauty, pushing ornaments to grow ever more elaborate. The males play a part in this, too, by accepting all females indiscriminately. As long as both sexes keep behaving the way they do, the genes for more elaborate tails will proliferate thanks to female preference, and genes for liking fancy tails will spread through the females. Any peahen that bucked the trend would end up nurturing unpopular sons who did little to help pass on her genes.

Sexual selection can also steer the evolution of females, especially in more monogamous species, but it doesn't tend to push them to extremes. The Brad Pitt of peacocks, after all, can make enough sperm to sire a new generation, but even a peahen as popular as Angelina Jolie would only be able to lay and incubate so many fertile eggs. If all the males in a flock mated only with her, the population could crash.

But peacocking is not simple for peacocks, or for humans. Beauty is hard to reduce to an algorithm. Mystery seemed to think he looked quite dazzling in his funny hat and jewelry. During our interview he told me he'd originally tried to call his book a guide to the "Venusian arts"—these being to love what martial arts are to fighting. Technically, "Venusian arts" would refer to art from the planet Venus—the equivalent of "Martian arts." If he wanted to name his techniques for the goddess Venus and the general field of love and sex, however, he'd have to use the unfortunate term "venereal arts," which might scare some people away.

Whatever you call the technique, it involves a display—a man has to demonstrate value to women. He has to be "a leader of men and a protector of loved ones." And he has to radiate self-assurance. Mystery then lowered his voice, telling me that while it's terribly politically incorrect to say so, "all women want to be dominated."

He was leaning in close, and I could see he wore beautifully applied eyeliner inside his lower lash line. I can never achieve that without smudging, I told him. He started to explain how he did it but stopped himself. "I'm not going to talk about makeup tips," he said. I wasn't sure if he was peacocking or peahenning, but apparently it works on other women.

THE PEACOCK'S TALE

Which brings up the age-old question: What do women want? This remains one of the great mysteries of science, along with the nature of consciousness and what happened before the big bang. It's a question the pickup artists are trying to answer for practical reasons, but it holds scientific interest because what women wanted over the eons literally shaped the male body and the male mind through sexual selection. Conversely, what men want also played a part in shaping women.

"I think it's a question every woman wonders about—how to find a really good mate," said biologist and peacock watcher Loyau. "We're attracted to people we don't really know. . . . Why this one and not that one?" We women often can't explain why one man catches our attention and lingers in our thoughts after a brief sighting or a few words.

Until recently, Loyau said, scientists didn't really understand what peahens want, either. Sure, they want a beautiful tail, but all males seem to have that, and many still don't get chosen. All the choices happen in a big gathering called a lek, where males fan out their feathers to display their tails while females look them over. "It's like a nightclub with lots of males dancing and females going to check out who would be the cutest," she said. Some males seem to get all the females, while most go away alone and rejected despite having what we humans would consider to be lovely tails.

A few years ago, she said, English scientists figured out that a female's choice is based on the number of eyespots the males show on their tails. That opened up another puzzle, said Loyau. A healthy, popular peacock can sport more than 270 spots, she said. His closest rivals might show a seemingly comparable 250 or 260 spots and get completely snubbed.

It seemed unlikely the peahens could count that high. To crack the mystery, Loyau started observing the peafowl in the Parc

Zoologique de Cleres, on the northern coast of France. Though the birds are really native to India, Pakistan, and Sri Lanka, they live as though wild in this park, she said.

Loyau found the length of a male's tail correlated with his place in the pecking order, the longest-tailed males reaching the upper rungs of the dominance hierarchy and staking out the biggest and most desirable territories. And yet length didn't matter to the females, who would often mate with shorter-tailed males if they had lots of spots. What could those peahens be thinking?

Loyau found that what mattered to females wasn't the sheer number of spots but the density. Approached by two males with the same number of spots, the female would choose the shorter-tailed one since he'd have to pack those spots closer together. Loyau went a step further to show this preference for spots was not some capricious and arbitrary whim on the part of the female but a decision that could mean life or death for her offspring. To sort out which peacocks were the most disease-resistant, Loyau injected them with a harmless vaccine designed to stimulate the birds' immune systems.

By later extracting and testing blood, she found the densely spotted males also boasted the strongest disease-fighting antibody responses. If she's right, then the peacock's tail is what scientists call a fitness indicator—an ornamental trait that serves as a proxy for something pertaining directly to the health and survival of the next generation.

Loyau found that peacocks also tend to beat each other up before the contests begin. "It's really bloody," she said. "They can be really violent. . . . I've even seen one male die from a fight." It's not at all clear who's ahead in love and life—peacocks or peahens. The males pay a heavy price for not building a nest or helping incubate the eggs or feeding the chicks. They often get beaten up trying to establish territory and status, and even after winning more fights than Russell Crowe in *Gladiator*, most still end up losing in the beauty pageant that lies at the focal point of their existence.

HUNG LIKE A FISH

The tail of a bird isn't the only thing that can grow to awkward proportions through sexual selection. The process also explains how a surprisingly large penis could be attached to a tiny creature—the lake-dwelling mosquito fish. This fish's plight shows that while some men would argue bigger is better, being too well-endowed can kill you.

The penis of the mosquito fish can extend to 70 percent of the length of his body, thereby interfering with his need to swim fast and escape deadly predators. There was no good explanation for why such a thing would evolve until a young biologist named Brian Langerhans took on the case. Langerhans, who works at Washington University in St. Louis, specializes in male organs. "It's an important field," he said. "For some reason male genitalia exhibit striking diversity in size and form, and naturalists sometimes have to look at the penis to tell one species from another."

In the case of the mosquito fish, the male's generous equipment makes him irresistible to females, said Langerhans. The downside is that the organ creates drag in the water, making the most well-endowed males easy pickings for predatory species.

Most fish don't have a penis at all—their idea of sex is to release sperm into the water. But a few fish do have intercourse and bear live young. For those species, the males need an organ for "sperm transfer," said Langerhans. Technically, it's called the gonodopo-dium, and it evolved independently from the penises of mammals, he said, though it's more or less the same thing.

Whatever you call it, there's no obvious reason it needs to be al-most as long as the fish itself. In fact, a male can only use a small portion of it in mating. Langerhans suspected that attraction had something to do with it. The mosquito fish penis might have grown so long because over the generations that's what females preferred. To test his hypothesis, he put female fish in a tank and projected pictures of male mosquito fish on the opposite sides. The pictures showed the same male, but in one Langerhans digitally extended the length of the penis by about 15 percent.

The females checked out both and then swam straight for the longer one every time, he said.

Could similar forces have shaped the male organs of other ani-mals, such as *Homo sapiens*? Author Jared Diamond argued that they did in his 1997 book *Why Is Sex Fun?* The average erect penis length of about five inches, Diamond wrote, is far more than a guy needs to procreate when our closest primate relatives get by with about one and a half inches. "The 1½ inch penis of the male orangutan permits it to perform in a variety of positions that rival ours . . . and to outperform us by executing all those positions while hanging from a tree."

Well, most of our relatives have small ones, with the glaring ex-ception of a rare African primate known as the bonobo. Nobody has done a formal survey of bonobo penis size, but primatologist Frans de Waal writes in his book *Our Inner Ape* that he suspects it beats the human one. And bonobos definitely use their penises for display: to attract attention (their form of peacocking), male bonobos spread their legs and use some well-developed muscle to wave their erections at females.

INTELLIGENT DESIGN?

In *The Mating Mind*, evolutionary psychologist Geoffrey Miller also argues that the human penis is a sexual ornament—or at least that its size was drastically increased thanks to female preference. Going the other way, he said, male choice may have endowed women with permanently swollen breasts. Like Darwin pondering those peacocks, I used to wonder how natural selection could have encumbered women this way, especially considering that for 99.99 percent of human existence there were no sports bras. Now I know.

In Miller's view, sexual selection was a major force in human evolution but has gone underappreciated by science and the general public. We tend to assume that our evolution was a deadly serious process driven strictly by survival needs. Sexual selection can seem instead to be powered by whimsy and personal aesthetics. Compared to natural selection, sexual selection seems downright frivolous. But there it is, shaping the forms of birds, reptiles, and almost certainly us humans.

Some scientists argue that our most elaborate sexual ornaments are in our heads. In Geoffrey Miller's view, creative intelligence, religion, and even morality are our peacock tails, with the all-important distinction that these traits evolved in women, too. That would explain the real Beatlemania. He equates sexual selection to a form of intelligent design, albeit one free from a supernatural creator. Men helped to design women and women to design men. So next time you complain that men are obtuse or women are unfathomable, remember who's to blame.

Some recent science would seem to back up Miller's contentions about creative intelligence. In 2005, psychologists at the University of Newcastle upon Tyne and the Open University determined that creative types do indeed experience more sexual variety, coupling with between four and ten partners in a lifetime compared to an average of three. The study's author, Daniel Nettle, attributed this to two possibilities: "It could be that very creative types lead a bohemian lifestyle and tend to act on more sexual impulses and opportunities," he said, "or they're considered to be very attractive and get lots of attention as a result."

There's a subtlety to Miller's argument that's easy to miss. It's trivial to say that creativity and musical talent are sexy. What he is proposing is different—namely, that these abilities evolved because they were considered sexy by our distant ancestors over hundreds of thousands of years. This picture challenges the commonly held paradigm in psychology that creativity came as a by-product of humanity's brain growth, which was initially propelled by the need for the practical skills involved in hunting.

Miller's argument relies on an emerging view of humanity's distant past that may differ from the one still held in the popular consciousness. In recent years archaeologists and anthropologists have come to realize that prehistoric human life was not a constant fight or flight or a mad scrabble for food. In the newer picture, our ancestors probably lived much like modern hunter-gatherers, most of whom get plenty of food and work only around four hours a day finding and preparing it.

Miller said the most important features of human evolution

emerged during the Pleistocene era, which began about 1.6 million years ago, when we were starting to look and act somewhat human. During that time, he said, our African ancestors were among the bigger animals on the savanna. You add our tendency to run in packs and use tools and you have one well-adapted primate. And so for the last million years or so, humans have been periodically wrestling with boredom.

In this newer picture, females didn't need as much provisioning or protection as previously thought. "Female hominids seem unlikely to have displayed the exaggerated physical vulnerability expected of women under patriarchy," Miller wrote. "When you picture ancestral females facing predators, do not imagine Marilyn Monroe whimpering and cowering. Imagine Steffi Graf brandishing a torch in place of a tennis racket." Our female ancestors may have chosen big, strong men not because we needed them to be that way but because we liked the look. And being self-sufficient and capable, our female ancestors could also afford to choose men who could tell a good story or joke, or could hold a riveting conversation, or sing.

Unlike the process in peacocks, sexual selection endows both men and women with these ornaments. That's because we're somewhat more monogamous than peacocks and men are choosy about women when it comes to long-term relationships at least. We're not totally symmetrical, though: men are slightly more likely than women to reproduce with multiple mates. They're also more likely to miss the chance to reproduce at all.

Miller and other evolutionary psychologists call our system a "market model." The way it works is that the most desirable man in the tribe gets the most desirable woman. The second most desirable man also wants the most desirable woman but he has to settle for the second best woman. The advantage to being near the top comes from the idea that our desirable traits act as a proxy for "good" genes that pass health on to our offspring. Those at the top get to pool their "good" genes with someone of equally "good" genes, thus increasing the odds they'll beget more and healthier children than almost everyone else. And those children are likely to make healthy grandchildren.

Rob Kurzban, an evolutionary psychologist at the University of Pennsylvania, has done some experiments to probe how human beings really chose mates. Kurzban said that for years there was some debate over whether we humans employed such a "market" system in which everyone agrees who's the most desirable or whether we instead used a seemingly kinder, gentler system called assortative mating. In the latter, which Kurzban refers to as the "Disney" model, we all seek different traits in our special matches. Thus, in assortative mating, an ugly green ogre really prefers an ugly green ogress over a beautiful princess.

To conduct his tests, Kurzban co-opted that popular option for meeting mates known as speed dating. At these events, a dozen or so each of men and women are brought together and rotate through a series of four-minute interviews, or conversations, until all the men have met all the women. Then they write down all their prospective matches that they'd like to see again. If there's any mutual interest, the organizers bring them together.

Kurzban found that reality conforms less to the Disney model and more to the market model, in which everyone agrees who's the most attractive and in the end we're forced to settle for the best we can get. That explains why Cyrano pined for beautiful Roxanne instead of falling for a woman with a giant proboscis. Of course, in the story, Cyrano's creative wit could have made him the prime peacock in town if only he could bring himself to fan his intellectual feathers for Roxanne. But in the story he gave his best feathers away to his rival Christian and walked away a loser.

But there's more to love and sex than beauty. Too bad Cyrano didn't know about pickup artists' boot camp. There, he and Christian could have learned how to be each other's wingmen.

11. ALPHA AND BETA

SEX, POWER, AND THE DECLINE
OF THE ALPHA MALE

Back at pickup artists' boot camp, the concept of the alpha male came up repeatedly. Partway through the seminar, for example, I finally realized what was so odd about the instructor's shoes. The treads were as thick as the wedges on my highest platform sandals. "Future" admitted as much, and said the shoes elevated him from a middling five feet ten to a little over six feet one, thereby making him much more alpha.

Those three inches matter, said Future, and science may back him up. In a 2007 *New York Times* column, writer John Tierney cited a study showing that a guy of five feet eight would have to make $146,000 a year more than one who was six feet tall to attract the same number of dates. A guy who was five-two would have to make $277,000 more. The pickup class advised the students to make themselves more alpha, with stronger voices and, yes, platform shoes. But for safety reasons, they've also developed a procedure for avoiding conflict with other possibly bigger, stronger guys—what they call the AMOG, or alpha male of the group. The "Method" instructs would-be pickup artists to charm the AMOG.

Never ignore him. You have to convince the alpha male you're not trying to steal the woman he wants, or the women he's already dating. You pretend, at least at first, that you're much more interested in talking to *him*.

Do human alpha males really exist, or do we just have big, brawny guys? I asked Stanford neuroscientist and primate expert Robert Sapolsky, who said he had his doubts. In some other species, alpha males exercise a kind of power that goes beyond what you see in humans. In dogs and wolves, for example, everyone has a place in a hierarchy, from one to, say, twenty. Dog number one is the alpha male but he's constantly challenged by dog number two. In baboons, however, there's just the one alpha male who rules over a group of equally subordinate non-alpha males. The alpha baboon gets to enjoy being king for a stretch of time before a challenger takes him on. Other species employ yet more varied social structures. Often, Sapolsky said, alpha males need coalitional support from other males to keep their position. Sometimes they need the support of the females.

Human society is structured in a much more complicated and unpredictable way. "In general, I think there's nothing resembling dominance hierarchies, let alone alpha males, for a number of reasons," Sapolsky said. First, we humans tend to belong to multiple social circles. The guy who empties the trash for a big corporation might be a star DJ at night or dominate the company softball team. And in the animal world, true alpha males father many more offspring than their rivals, which is something we don't see in human beings.

But since scientists see alpha males in two of our closest relatives, gorillas and chimpanzees, I wondered whether humans and those other apes evolved from a common ancestor that did have alpha males. In our lineage, then, alpha males could be in the process of being phased out. Could this explain why men are still somewhat bigger than women? I asked Sapolsky. "That's an interesting question," he said. The average size differential between the sexes could have evolved because, among our distant ancestors, males did fight each other for the chance to monopolize more females. Scientists say that, in general, when you see bigger males it means they're forced to compete for sex through physical force or intimidation. Males are bigger in most mammal species—and are often armed with built-in weapons such as antlers or dangerous teeth. In our case, men weigh in at an average of 173 pounds and women 136, which makes men, on average, about 15 percent bigger than women, though the difference varies a bit by race.

That's a pretty modest difference considering that gorilla males weigh twice as much as their females. Chimp males, like human ones, are only modestly bigger than the females, but they have huge, deadly canine teeth not shared by the female. "It's very well understood what those teeth are for," said Tim White, an anthropologist at the University of California, Berkeley, and a widely known expert on human evolution. White said it's likely that alpha males ruled the common ape ancestors that humans shared with chimps some 7 million years ago, but in our lineage they've all but disappeared as men and women have grown more monogamous and more alike. If that's the case, how did such a transformation happen? And when?

LUCY'S BOYFRIEND

One of the hottest points of contention in human evolution centers on the time about 3.2 million years ago, which is just about halfway between the chimp/human split and today. Back then, Africa was populated by diminutive, upright-walking creatures called *Australopithecus afarensis*. The best-known of these is Lucy, whose skeleton was found in Ethiopia in 1974. Her discoverers named her after the Beatles song "Lucy in the Sky with Diamonds," which the anthropologists were reportedly listening to when they found her.

White said if you saw Lucy alive today, you'd probably run for the hills. Fierce and strong like our ape relatives, she was only marginally smarter than a chimp, yet she walked upright like a human being. From a long distance you might think she was a human child, he said. Most scientists agree Lucy was a female, though there remain a few dissenters. But how big were males of her species compared to females? The long-prevailing story was laid out in the 1980s by Kent State University anthropologist Owen Lovejoy. Putting together the few fragmentary bones of Lucy-type creatures, he deduced that the males were only slightly bigger— just like modern men and women. Lucy's male counterparts had also lost the big canines that show up in chimps and older human ancestors.

This suggested that by 3.2 million years ago the pressure was off these hominid males to beat each other up or impress their peers with pure brawn. Our male ancestors had started developing a new mating strategy to get females. Lovejoy uses the term monogamy but not necessarily of the mate-once-for-life variety. "Monogamy is a loaded term," said White. The smaller, less fanged males may have bonded with females and even lent a hand to feeding the offspring, but like members of many other officially monogamous species, they probably cheated a bit or practiced serial monogamy. Other anthropologists dispute Lovejoy, arguing that Lucy's male counterparts were much larger. It all depends on how you analyze the bones, said White. If you took a hundred gorilla skeletons, there would be small female ones and large male ones and nothing in between. If you looked at a hundred human skeletons, however, you'd see some large ones and some small and many in between, since some women are larger than some men. You also see many in-between members among the remains of Lucy's species, said White. Given such an ambiguous situation, it's not surprising that another faction in the anthropology community argues for a much larger sex differential, more like modern gorillas, thus implying Lucy's males still beat each other up in order to secure the alpha position and get most of the sex.

More fossils may finally settle the question of when in our lineage the alpha males were deposed in favor of more monogamous and more fatherly ones. Stanford University anthropologist Richard Klein, author of *The Dawn of Human Culture*, says that whatever way the Lucy debate turns out, our ancestral line probably acquired our current size differential by at least 1.7 to 1.8 million years ago. Around that point our ancestors were classified under our current genus, *Homo*, though not yet of the species *Homo sapiens*. But even in these more recent human predecessors, the fossil evidence is still sketchy, according to White. In *Homo habilis*, for example, the males appear much bigger, but some scientists suspect they're really looking not at two sexes but at two different species, White said. "These things don't come labeled."

Can we infer anything about humanity's natural mating strategy from our current size differential? As a general rule, in very monogamous species, such as penguins and certain monkeys, males and females grow to exactly the same size. And in species in which males collect many females, such as gorillas and sea lions, males tend to grow much bigger. "What becomes clear is we're halfway in between," said Stanford biologist Sapolsky. And so what's not clear is how we evolved to mate. Cross-cultural studies and casual observations reveal the same thing—men are all over the map. Some mate once, for life, some go through a series of spouses, some choose one main mate and a few mistresses, and then there's the guy who had sex with more than 200 women and, still not satisfied, signed up for Seduction Boot Camp.

WHAT'S WRONG WITH THOSE MALES?

Some humans are looking for clues to our own nature in that of our two closest living relatives—the chimpanzee and the bonobo. Bonobos are much rarer than chimpanzees and are best known for their playful bisexual encounters. The two species also divvy up power very differently.

In groups of chimpanzees, one male will rise to the alpha position through violence or even murder and will use his power to monopolize females and sometimes food. But heavy hangs the head that wears the crown, as a bloody coup is always around the corner. In his 2005 book *Our Inner Ape,* primatologist Frans de Waal describes some horrifying incidents involving zoo chimpanzees, including one fight in which a pair of male chimps held down the alpha male of the group and clawed his testicles out.

Though they're less well studied than chimpanzees, bonobos are equally closely related to human beings. A common ancestor of bonobos and chimpanzees split from our lineage around 7 million years ago. Many bonobo watchers say these animals much more closely resemble us than do chimps—in gait, facial features, and behavior. In a film shown at a science writers' convention I attended a few years ago, a group of zoo bonobos were busy giving each other surprisingly human-like renditions of oral and manual sex.

What some human males seem to find even more shocking about bonobos is that the males let the females dominate them. This is what happens in captivity, at least. Scientists know little of the behavior of wild bonobos because their numbers are few, between 6,000 and 100,000, and because they're confined to a small region of the Congo. The experts disagree over how much their captive behavior really reveals, but for the next few years it represents the bulk of our knowledge of them.

And their behavior is striking in that male bonobos cede power to females even though they have a size advantage comparable to that of the human male. They also have dangerous canine fangs that their female counterparts lack. The females generally assume the upper hand by banding together, said de Waal. If there's food around, females will start eating it, forcing males to "beg" for a portion. The ranking in a bonobo troop starts with the alpha female and then descends through all the females, placing the top male below the bottom female.

To make matters worse, de Waal wrote, that top male gets his position not through his own cunning or strength but through the rank and political machinations of his mother.

In his book, de Waal recounted how, when describing this bonobo hierarchy at a big scientific meeting, a German researcher could stand it no longer, jumping out of his seat to cry out, "What's wrong with those males?" But bonobos are not all peace and love, he said. Males are still competitive, vying for chances to mate, and they sometimes get beaten up by gangs of females, but he maintains that their scuffles don't come close to the vicious attacks perpetrated by male chimps.

Which relative do we resemble more? It's a hard question, since chimpanzees, bonobos, and humans have all evolved in different directions and we don't know much about the common ancestor we all share. But bonobos still offer us humans the hope that we're not necessarily hardwired for murder, war, power struggles, and male domination.

WHY ALPHAS DON'T ALWAYS WIN

Being a beta male in a species with alphas doesn't mean you have to sit out the mating game. For those who just don't have the size or the strength, there's still the life of the "sneaker." These are males that slip in to mate while Mr. Alpha is busy fighting or mating with another female. Some male salmon sneak, as do blue-gilled sunfish, certain male reptiles, and a few mammals. Sneakers can be born to their fate through genetics, or, in other cases, environmental cues may allow them to switch between sneaking and other strategies. (The official scientific term for this type of male is "sneaky fucker," coined by the eminent British biologist John Maynard Smith.)

Peter Rodman, a retired professor from the University of California, Davis, who studies orangutans, said adult males come in two completely different forms: a sneaker who grows to about the same size as the female and an alpha male who grows to twice as big. The smaller males live low-profile lives, furtively engaging in the occasional tryst with a female. These sneakers may go on this way indefinitely, or, if one of the big males somehow dies or disappears, a sneaker male's hormones will trigger a huge growth spurt and he'll metamorphose into an alpha male. Among sneaker males of various other species, one popular strategy is to look exactly like a female. The upside is you can hang out with the females all day long and the alpha male won't try to kill you. The downside is he may occasionally mount you.

Something even more complicated than this happens in the hills of central California, where naturalists discovered three distinct types of males in one species—the side-blotched lizard. The males of this lizard species even come conveniently color-coded in yellow, orange, and blue. "That had to mean something," said biologist Barry Sinervo of the University of California, Santa Cruz. After about five years of stalking them, he said, he thinks he finally figured it out. The orange lizards are the alpha males—"big bruisers who fight over territory." The yellow ones look just like the females, so they're the classic female-mimic sneakers. The females don't seem to mind the effeminate look of the yellows, so these guys still get lots of sex. Harder to explain were the blue males. They weren't big enough to fight off the alpha males, nor could they fool the alphas like the transvestite yellow ones. But the blue males did get sex, and Sinervo watched them long enough to see how they managed it.

It turns out they employ one of the most popular techniques taught by the seduction gurus and known to many single men beyond the so-called pickup community. They pair up, one male getting the girl and the other playing wingman. Among humans, the wingman can do many important jobs—entertaining and diverting rivals, or, more often, entertaining a desired woman's female friends. For lizards, the job of the wingman is to chase away the sneaker yellow males. The blue males never cheat on each other, Sinervo said. The one that plays the wingman is ever loyal. "The blue male will give up his life for another blue male."

But even paired with a wingman the blue males still can't beat up the alpha males, he said. That turns the competition for sex among these three kinds of male lizards into a game of rock-paper-scissors. The yellow males can triumph over the orange alphas by their sneaking. The blue males can triumph over the yellow sneakers through cooperation; but since they aren't in disguise like the yellows, blues tend to lose out to the orange lizards, who are bigger and meaner. That kind of pattern shows up in a few other species, Sinervo said, but what's really rare in nature is the altruism shown by the blue wingmen. Nonhuman animals rarely sacrifice themselves unless they stand to gain in some other way or to benefit close relatives. In the human animal, too, we often expect to see payback for our favors. But the game of sex follows more complex rules than does the game of survival.

In species with no male-male fighting or alpha males, it can benefit a male to be smaller than the female. A smaller male doesn't need as much food, for one thing. Males are smaller than females in many species of insects, fish, amphibians, and reptiles. The world's record for largest male-female size gap, as recorded in the *Guiness Book of World Records,* goes to the deep-sea anglerfish— a.k.a. the sea devil. In that species the female is a whopping 500,000 times the size of the male, by weight. The females stretch to about five feet long, while the males resemble gnats. The scientist responsible for discovering the male of the species, Ted Pietsch of the University of Washington, Seattle, said the males in this case really are parasitic. When a male anglerfish finds a mate, he bites her, digs in, and attaches himself permanently. Then he starts living off her blood. It's hard to fathom how that could be good for her, but at least you can't say the male fears intimacy.

Human males are unlikely to keep shrinking that far, even if alpha males continue to be phased out of existence. For one thing, surveys show that women like bigger men, so as long as we keep choosing them, men could easily stay bigger than women. Beyond that, women have grown to depend on men to help raise and provide for children, and you need to keep up a certain minimum size to do that. Male animals that tend to help with the babies usually grow to the same size as females and often look just like them, say the scientists. We may be evolving in that direction.

12. WHO'S YOUR DADDY?

FATHERLY MALES AND THE
SEX APPEAL OF MR. MOM

When asked what allowed human beings to expand around the world, leaving other apes behind, most people would credit intelligence, language, hunting skills, fire, or manual dexterity. But there's another factor, perhaps even more elemental, that separates human beings from all our ape relatives. It's the human male capacity to care, both for females and for children.

Male apes do little or nothing to care for the young they may spawn, leaving all the work to the females, which means female chimpanzees and bonobos must wait for four or five years between births. With the help of male mates, human females can give birth more often. And yet, fatherly behavior remains a bit puzzling.

From an evolutionary standpoint, there's a big downside to being a good father, said anthropologist Eduardo Fernandez-Duque of the University of Pennsylvania. The problem is that most male animals can't know for sure which babies, if any, are really theirs. That makes them vulnerable to being cuckolded. Caring for another male's offspring will send a nice guy's genes into oblivion while helping those of the interloping rival to spread and flourish.

One way to minimize that ever-present doubt over paternity is monogamy. And, indeed, monogamy and fatherliness go together like babies and diapers. In harsh environments, where babies need intense care and protection to survive, parenting plus monogamy may make the best male strategy. When that's the case, the most charming, big, tough, funny, or promiscuous males don't pass on their genes unless they stick around to help their progeny survive. So it's the fatherly males that end up prevailing, as long as they stick by their mates or otherwise prevent them from cheating.

PENGUIN LOVE

If you want a harsh environment, you can't get much worse than the frozen continent of Antarctica, home to one of the world's shining examples of paternal care—the emperor penguin. Male penguins of this species seem to endure the worst of all possible worlds—almost nonexistent sex lives that nonetheless lead them to parenthood, total self-sacrifice, and endless suffering.

Not surprisingly, when their lifestyle was popularized in the 2004 documentary film *March of the Penguins,* conservative commentators cheered. "It demonstrated qualities of sacrifice and devotion and the importance of child rearing and bringing the next generation into the world," said Michael Medved, host of a conservative radio talk show in Seattle. He said this was the first movie many of his listeners had seen since *The Passion of the Christ.* Other conservatives, such as *National Review* editor Rich Lowry, also publicly extolled the film and set up the penguins as paragons of family values.

The French-made film, narrated by Morgan Freeman, became the second-highest grossing documentary of all time. To briefly summarize the plot, scores of emperor penguins leap from the sea and march for miles to some frigid inland wasteland where the temperature drops to 80 degrees below zero. They pick mates and lay eggs. The dads dutifully incubate the eggs for weeks, fasting and suffering through blizzards. The moms suffer as they search for food, the parents both suffer and sacrifice as they feed their hatchlings, and some mother penguins lose their young and wail and cry. They live for nothing but their children. It's called a love story.

But men shouldn't worry too much if they can't live up to this ideal. Luckily for the penguins, it's really not quite that bad. Scientists say the documentary people indulged in a bit of exaggeration, or perhaps poetic license. For one thing, it's not minus 80 out there. It's minus 40 at the worst, said Gerald Kooyman, a penguin expert from the Scripps Institution of Oceanography in La Jolla, California. "Why would they exaggerate that?" asked Kooyman, who has made more than a dozen trips to Antarctica. Kooyman said these penguins probably aren't suffering nearly as much as we humans would under the circumstances, since they're much better adapted to the cold.

Viewers are told that a pair of young penguins who fumble and lose their egg have suffered an intolerable loss. But how do we know their squeaks aren't just penguin for something like "Oops. Oh well. Hey, let's get something to eat"? And that tearful scene when a "mother" is shown wailing over her frozen chick? Kooyman suspects it was staged.

While some conservative commentators praised the penguins for being monogamous, it turns out emperor penguins practice the Rudy Guiliani version: they don't mate for life but instead go with a series of different mates. Not that there was much actual mating in the film; mostly the penguins nuzzled. If you watched carefully, though, you could see one lying on its tummy while another stood behind it—that was penguin sex. But it would be jumping to conclusions to assume the female was the prone one.

In fact, scientists are mystified as to how the penguins themselves figure out which sex they are, said John Rowden, a curator at the Central Park Zoo. To humans they're identical, even if you look between their penguin legs, where they all sport an opening called a cloaca. When opposite-sex penguins rub their nether regions together, the male squirts semen from his cloaca into hers. In zoos, genetic tests can distinguish the sexes, which is how curators at Central Park discovered that some of their penguins were gay—or at least having gay sex. "We currently have a number of same-sex pairs," Rowden says. Biologists say same-sex pair bonding happens in ducks and geese as well as a number of other birds. Given the situation with penguins it's impossible to tell whether any of the birds in the film were boy-boy or girl-girl couples that stole or adopted eggs.

While birds are more likely to show paternal care and practice monogamy than mammals, several monkeys stand out as praiseworthy by the standards of the family-values gang. Titi monkeys of the Amazon rain forest, for example, mate for life, the mated pairs perching on branches side by side, their tails intertwined. And just as those fatherly male penguins are hard to tell from females, so titi monkey males are indistinguishable from their partners.

When a baby monkey is born, the father almost instantly picks it up and starts carrying it around, passing it back to the mother to feed. The babies usually prefer riding on the father, say the scientists who study them, even when the mother's mammary glands hold the source of all meals.

So strong is this father-offspring bond that if a baby in a captive group gets sick and has to go to the veterinary hospital, the scientists say you always send Dad, or at least another male, along. When separated from their fathers, baby titi monkeys secrete lots of cortisol—a classic symptom of the separation anxiety that normally afflicts mammal babies separated from their mothers. The love is a bit lopsided, say the researchers, since adult titi monkeys get much more upset when separated from their mates than they do when separated from their kids.

Titi monkeys also make good stepparents, said UC Davis's Peter Rodman, another monkey watcher. He found that these monkeys take up new mates if one dies—something that happens fairly often in a forest crawling with animals that like to eat monkeys.

Rodman and his colleagues don't have enough cases yet to draw any sweeping conclusions, but in a couple of instances they witnessed the death of a mother or father and the integration of a stepparent into the family. If you didn't know, he said, you'd never guess the new mom or dad wasn't the biological one.

In other animals, males will often kill the infants of a single mother or widow. For some, infanticide helps them pass on their genes since new mothers are less fertile while they lactate. Killing the babies causes them to ovulate again. Why would titi monkeys be so different, helping babies that aren't biologically theirs? One possibility, Rodman said, is the troops are so closely related the new male may be a brother or cousin of the biological father. In that case, acting as stepfather still helps pass some of his genes into posterity.

I asked Rodman if the titi monkeys were acting on paternal instinct. "Instinct is just a way of describing what your hormones do to you," he said. In mammals, he said, what you feel as instinctive behavior may be induced by oxytocin, vasopressin, prolactin, or testosterone. To better understand the role of hormones in parenting, he pointed me to psychologist Karen Bales, also at UC Davis, who's worked with the little rodents called voles.

Voles come in several different species, each with very different male behaviors. Male meadow voles just try to get laid as much as possible. Male prairie voles tend to fall in love when they mate, and as soon as babies arrive, they perform all the same parental behaviors the females do—licking, cleaning, grooming, and fussing over them. The difference, she said, all comes down to the distribution of molecules in the voles' brains. Oxytocin and vasopressin both work by attaching to other molecules, called receptors, which are distributed differently in the brains of prairie and meadow voles. In the late 1990s, researchers decided to add some extra oxytocin and vasopressin receptors to the brains of the no-strings-attached promiscuous meadow voles. The altered brain chemistry induced these Don Juans of the rodent world to commit to one female. Bales said she also suspected these same hormones influence male-offspring bonding. So she took the naturally parental male prairie voles and blocked their ability to absorb vasopressin and oxytocin. She said she had to block both hormones to turn the family values prairie voles into deadbeat dads. If you just blocked one hormone, the other would compensate.

But the connection between fatherly care and monogamy isn't

as simple as it might look, said Duke University anthropologist Susan Alberts, who studies baboons in Kenya. Baboons aren't monogamous at all, she said. The females go into heat and mate with as many males as they can get away with. The males will try to monopolize females during the five-day periods when the females are fertile, with varying degrees of success, Alberts said. But there's still no way any male baboon could know which babies came from his sperm Alberts said.

And yet, when babies are born, a purported father will come forward and volunteer to carry them around, protecting them from predators and helping them get from tree to tree. Male baboons don't expend as much energy parenting as titi monkeys, but they still do an impressive job for non-monogamous animals.

Are they just guessing or do they somehow sense which babies are theirs? "My working hypothesis is males have several potential cues, none of which is very accurate but they combine them," she said. It may be a combination of pheromones and the memory of mating with a female during her fertile time. It's not that baboons know sex leads to reproduction, she said. "It's something much less logic-based."

While I was covering the 2007 meeting of the American Association of Physical Anthropologists held in Philadelphia, I came across a whole session devoted to the evolution of fathering. There, a big point of contention surrounded the link between fathering and hunting. In most foraging cultures, men spend a big chunk of their time and energy hunting. Is that part of being a good father? Or is it the opposite—a show-off tactic meant to help get a little action on the side?

"The question is, are men hunting to provision their kids or is it just a way of showing off to others what a badass you are," said anthropologist Michael Gurven of the University of California, Santa Barbara. The logic behind the show-off theory is that if men were really driven to help their own kids—say, to the extent that penguins are—they'd go after more reliable sources of food, such as plants and small game—as foraging women do. But instead they bring back big animals that have to be shared or they'll rot, thus catching the attention of other women. Hunting, then, is not really about bringing home the bacon; it's about what the scientists call "mating effort"—something akin to the pickup artists' peacocking. The upshot, said Gurven, is that "men are pigs and hunter-gatherers are just like guys everywhere."

But Gurven isn't ready to buy that sentiment, especially after spending months living with a foraging group in Bolivia called the Tsimane. The 8,000 remaining Tsimane make up one of the few peoples who still depend on hunting and gathering for food. The men kill wild pigs, monkeys, and tapirs. They try to get most of the meat to their own families, he said. And when they share, it buys them points with other hunters, who will reciprocate later when a man is sick or having a run of bad luck. "It's like an insurance policy," he said.

He and his graduate student Jeffrey Winking found that the more kids these men already had, the harder they worked at hunting. And he said hunting may do more overall good for a family where the mother and older children are already gathering those reliable but less protein-rich fruits and wild potatoes. Hunting may carry high risks, but it offers high potential returns for the family, he said—though if a man gets a reputation as a badass hunter, it serves as a nice fringe benefit. Among the Tsimane, hunting skill is what women want, he said. "There are a lot of different things going on. It's not as simple as just impressing women versus feeding more kids."

This question of men's intentions pervades anthropology circles, said Frank Marlowe of Florida State University. He's considered the question while living in Tanzania with a group called the Hadza. In that group it's customary for the men to live in huts with their wives and children, and to help out with the parenting. "It's funny that some claim the nuclear family is a Western invention," he said, when it's common around the world. Still, the Hadza allow no-fault divorce, and they make good use of day care. Once kids reach three or four, parents leave them in a big group where they're looked after by a single adult, the arrangement freeing both men and women to go about their business.

For men, that business is hunting big animals. And while Hadza men will sometimes appear to be sharing their kills with the whole group, Marlowe said, over time he learned it didn't quite work that way. "It's just that it's hard to bring an impala back into the village without people coming out and taking some," he said. Hadza people act like many of us do when we're visiting very close friends or family members—we help ourselves to food.

So rather than show off their kills, he said, men often try to hide them and sneak them home. "Men really do care about provisioning their families." But of course the best hunters earn admiration from other women, so he's not taking sides in the show-off versus provider debate, he said. "It's a little of both."

For his part, University of Pennsylvania anthropologist Eduardo Fernandez-Duque said he'd like to see more research on the effects of fatherly care. What does it mean for child development? Family stability? So much research now targets women and the question of their working rather than staying home with kids. He'd like to do some of that research himself, he said, if he wasn't so busy. He's got three sons to help raise, after all.

SEX AND THE SINGLE FATHER

In humans, direct fatherly care is just plain sexy. We women go all mushy over men holding babies or even pushing baby carriages. In evolutionary terms, the more women find it sexy, the more fatherly males will get to pass on their fatherly genes. According to one recent study, women are so attuned to fatherhood potential that they can tell whether a man likes kids by just looking at him.

In 2006, researchers reported that they took a group of thirty-nine male college students and tested their interest in children by showing them pairs of pictures—one of a baby or child under about six and one of an adult. By asking which photos the men preferred to look at, they estimated their subjects' baby interest, said University of Chicago biology professor Dario Maestripieri. Some chose all babies, he said; others chose all adults, and still others, a mix. Then the scientists snapped neutral-expression headshots of the men and showed them to undergraduate women, asking the women to rate each man's interest in children.

"We were surprised," he said, that the men flagged by the women as probably liking children were the same men who tended to prefer the baby pictures. The scientists also measured testosterone levels and found that women reacted to this too, but in a different way. When asked whom they'd like for a short-term hook-up, said Maestripieri, the women chose the men with high testosterone, "but for the long term, they picked the guys who liked babies."

If you're one of those guys who would have picked the pictures of the adults, you can at least take heart that you're better off than certain male fish. In some species, a male can't get as much as a look from a female unless he's already devotedly tending little fish larvae. For many fish, "being fatherly seems to be a strong signal to the female to mate," said Mark Sabaj, an ichthyologist at the Academy of Natural Sciences in Philadelphia. It poses a big catch-22 if you have to be a father to become a father. How can a guy break in? In some species, such as sticklebacks, males will steal eggs from other males. In one type of minnow, said Sabaj, a male will oust a rival from his nest, treating most of the other guy's eggs as caviar but leaving behind just enough to fool a female into thinking he's a nice single dad.

Another popular tactic is fakery. This, Sabaj suspects, might explain one weird-looking catfish he's seen in various South American waters. Called a bristlenose pleco, the female looks normal enough but the male sprouts dozens of wormlike tentacles from his head. Could the tentacles have evolved because females started mistaking them for fish larvae? A similar tactic almost worked for Hugh Grant's character when he borrowed a friend's child to help him score in the 2002 film *About a Boy*.

Other fish display fleshy yellow knobs or spots on their fins that look like eggs. So why not larvae? And the male bristlenose pleco is under pressure to look desirable since he has to be chosen by a female. Males stake out cavities in rocks and wait like eager young debutantes as the females swim by and inspect them. The females, ever paternity conscious, look for males tending larvae, or so they think. Once she makes her choice, a female enters a male's cavity, lays eggs all over the walls, and leaves. This may not sound like hot sex by our standards, but to them, apparently, this is as good as it gets.

For all his trouble, once the male fertilizes the eggs and becomes a real father, he ends up with all the parenting and housework. "He uses his fins and mouth to clean the eggs and clear the cavity of detritus . . . and aerates the clutch by fanning it with his pectoral fins," Sabaj wrote in a scientific paper he coauthored with Jonathan Armbruster and Lawrence Page. While a number of fish species put the parenting burden on the fathers, others dump everything on the mothers, Sabaj says, and in still others, nobody does anything but release sperm and eggs.

Sex and reproduction can drive the evolution of the beautiful, the strange, and the impractical. With so much pressure on sexual species to mate, it seems a bit mysterious that some people completely rebel through homosexuality and various other forms of gender-bending. When it comes to alternative forms of sexuality, human beings are far from alone in seeming to break all the rules.

13. SEXUAL OUTLAWS

HOMOSEXUALS, BISEXUALS, TRANSSEXUALS, AND THE POWER OF DIVERSITY IN THE GAME OF LIFE

Before the 2004 presidential election, George W. Bush was asked whether he thought homosexuality was a choice. His answer—he didn't know. "How could he not know?" I yelled at the television set. I didn't choose to feel attracted to men. It just happened. Unless the purportedly heterosexual Bush was really bisexual, he must have felt the same way about his attraction to women.

If sexual orientation is indeed rooted in our nature, however, homosexuality raises an interesting evolutionary question. In a world where evolution favors traits that advance reproduction, how could homosexuality continue to flourish? Is it just a rare aberration or a common mating pattern? Experts are still disputing the findings of sex research pioneer Alfred Kinsey, who shocked America in 1948 when he reported that a man's sexual orientation could point anywhere between gay and straight. In his *Sexual Behavior of the Human Male*, Kinsey stated that 10 percent of American men surveyed were exclusively homosexual for at least three years between the ages of sixteen and fifty-five and a whopping 37 percent of men reported at least one homosexual experience. An even higher percentage reported some degree of sexual attraction to other men.

Kinsey's findings were often interpreted to say that our culture pushes men to adopt either a straight or gay posture—more often a straight one in 1940s America. For women between twenty and thirty-five, he found that only between 2 and 6 percent reported being "more or less exclusively homosexual in experience/response." Over the years, Kinsey's claims have been widely disputed. Some critics accused Kinsey of relying too heavily on prison inmates to gather his data—thus failing to represent the American public at large. But the crux of his finding was beyond dispute—many Americans were doing it with members of their own sex and quite a few were exclusively gay. More recent statistics put the percentage of gay men between 2 and 5 percent of the American population—very close to what Kinsey observed for women.

How much influence does culture wield in our sexual behavior and orientation? The ancient Greeks showed it can go pretty far. In Plato's *Symposium*, written around 385 B.C., male characters extol the virtues of male-male love, especially between men and young "boys" (teens). The setting for Plato's work is a sort of drinking party where various speakers—Plato's real contemporaries—hold forth on the nature of erotic love.

Aristophanes, the comic poet and playwright, for example, says we fall in love because we were once complete spherical creatures, some all male, some all female, and some half and half. Then, as a punishment for some transgression, the gods split us all apart. So your sexual orientation depends on the sex of your original other half.

Later in the party, the philosopher Socrates claims that male-male love is more elevated, purer, and deeper than male-female love. Was Socrates really talking about gay love or just "platonic" love between buddies?

It was pretty gay, according to Simon Goldhill, who clarifies much of Greek culture for the laymen in his book *Love, Sex and Tragedy*. In Goldhill's view, the Greeks of Plato's era were both widely homosexual and at the same time homophobic. They despised gay men who didn't follow their society's strict rules of homosexual courtship and sex. An honorable relationship, for example, could only take place between a grown man and a teenage boy. The teenage boy should be tall and muscular but not old enough to grow a full beard. It was as if the encounter didn't count as gay as long as one of the men was young and hairless.

Male lovers usually met in the gymnasium, which, according to Goldhill, was not all that different from our gyms today. Men went there to network and improve their physiques, though in ancient Greece they worked out naked.

If everyone was following protocol, the older man was supposed to court the younger one, buying him gifts and offering him mentorship and guidance. The young man was supposed to act coy, only allowing the most worthy suitors to romance him. Once he consented, a respectable boy knew to limit the sex to certain sanctioned acts. The man and the teenage boy could kiss and touch and the older man would then put his penis between the boy's thighs and rub it back and forth, in what Goldhill terms intercrucial intercourse. To illustrate how accepted this was, Goldhill included in his book pictures of vases and drinking vessels on which artists had painted naked or partly clad males engaged in this type of sex. In one, the older man sports an obvious erection, and though he appears to fondle the boy's genitalia, the boy never becomes aroused, as was considered proper. The boy wasn't supposed to rub his own penis between the man's thighs. He gave pleasure, and the older man received it.

Despite their open embrace and artistic celebration of this type of male-male sex, and the tolerant view of Aristophanes, most Greeks mocked or even abhorred grown men who had sex with other grown men, calling them *cinaidos*—the meanest epithet a Greek man could hurl at his fellow man. "It's the sort of high-octane insult that can't even be a joke," wrote Goldhill. Men were not supposed to be effeminate in their dress or behavior, and the Greeks considered oral and anal sex to be disgusting acts if they were done between two men.

Greeks also looked down on youths who were too easily seduced or who chased after older men. Near the end of the *Symposium*, the Greek politician Alcibiades described his own unrequited love for Socrates. As a young man, Alcibiades had been considered extraordinarily beautiful, while Socrates was older and considered ugly but extraordinarily wise. Though Socrates was said to have a yen for attractive youths, the comely Alcibiades could not win him over and eventually resorted to chasing the old philosopher. Socrates rejected the young man's advances, perhaps seeing him as too much of a social climber.

Alcibiades later proved a corrupt politician and was exiled for treason, according to Goldhill, who reflected that his life might have turned out differently had he won over the great Socrates and secured his love and guidance.

THE GENETICS OF DESIRE

When I asked geneticist Dean Hamer whether he thought homosexuality was a choice, he gave a much clearer answer than did Mr. Bush. Hamer told me he never chose to be attracted to men. As we talked inside the sleekly renovated Washington, D.C., townhouse he shared with his partner and two dogs, the scientist popularly associated with so-called gay genes said he had known he was gay since he was about five.

That's what partly motivated Hamer to switch from basic molecular genetics to the study of sexual orientation back in 1992. When he told his colleagues at the National Cancer Institute what he was doing, they were puzzled. "It was pretty far out there," he said. Others, being geneticists, thought the answer was too obvious to warrant scientific investigation: of course sexual orientation was genetic.

But outside the scientific community, Hamer said, it's still widely believed that gay people somehow choose their orientation and this belief further fuels discrimination. Hamer's critics—and he has many—question whether a scientific analysis of sexual orientation will help foster tolerance and understanding or simply give new ammunition to the homophobes and bigots. Some pundits warn that identifying a "gay gene" will encourage, or at least allow, expectant parents to use it for selective abortion. "That scares some straight people away from studying this," said Hamer. "They're afraid of offending someone or causing harm."

Hamer said he was influenced by several studies in the late 1980s, especially one that focused on twins—a standard genetics technique. The thinking goes that if a trait is shared more often by identical twins than by fraternal twins, it means genes influence the trait to some extent. That's because identical twins carry the same genetic code while fraternal twins, like ordinary siblings, share half their genes. For men, if one identical twin is gay, there's about a fifty-fifty chance the other will be gay, too. That falls to about 20 percent if they're fraternal twins. (For women, studies show there's a genetic component to sexual orientation as well.)

On reading the twin studies, Hamer reasoned he might be able to use the tools from his field of molecular genetics to isolate specific genes associated with homosexuality. He therefore took DNA samples from forty pairs of gay brothers, seeking genetic patterns they had in common. What he found was not a specific gene but what's called a marker. The term refers to any spelling difference in genetic codes that shows up on DNA tests. When scientists find such a spelling variation associated with a trait, it means any number of genes that lie near that marker on a chromosome might be responsible, since genes are inherited in clumps.

The marker that Hamer identified was on the X chromosome, in a region called Xq28. That meant a gay gene might reside anywhere in this particular genetic neighborhood. Here it might help to briefly review the relevant patterns of inheritance. Men get one copy of the X chromosome from their mothers and a Y from their fathers. Women have two X chromosomes, and while these tend to exchange some genetic information, the region Xq28 usually gets passed down intact. So mothers pass each of their sons one of two possible Xq28s.

That means two brothers have a 50-percent chance of both inheriting the same piece of the X chromosome—Xq28—from their mother. If there were no genes in this part of the X that influenced homosexuality, then about half of the pairs of gay brothers would still share that same region by chance, just as would happen with forty randomly chosen pairs of brothers.

Instead, Hamer found that thirty-three of the forty sets of gay brothers shared this same piece of the X chromosome. The findings implied that a gene in this region had some influence on sexual orientation. When Hamer first published this result in 1993, Xq28 became known as the gay gene, but he insists the resulting sound bites vastly oversimplified the science. Any gene in that region shared by the gay brothers would also be shared by many straight men and would not be enough, on its own, to cause homosexual orientation.

A subsequent study claimed men with several older brothers were more likely to be gay, but that result was often interpreted in a misleading way. Since only about 2 to 5 percent of all men are gay according to surveys, men with two or three older brothers are only slightly more likely to be gay than anyone else. Even a man with three or four older brothers is still much more likely to be straight than gay.

Only a few studies attempted to replicate Hamer's X chromosome finding, and those tended to refute it. In *Evolution's Rainbow*, biologist Joan Roughgarden wrote that these follow-up studies may not have agreed with Hamer's original work because scientists were using different questions to identify gay men. Hamer and colleagues asked men whether they felt homosexual "at the core," while a follow-up study in Canada, for example, asked only about homosexual behavior. "I support conventional wisdom," wrote Roughgarden, "which is suspicious of any result highly dependent on how a question is posed."

To Hamer, the question of a gay gene on the X remains unresolved. Most genetic findings are followed up by hundreds of similar studies, but the gay gene is not popular subject matter.

BI-OLOGY

When Hamer set out to study gay genetics, some of his critics pointed out that he might have overlooked bisexuality. But Hamer said all the men told him they were either completely straight or completely gay. None reported anything in between. Hamer and some other sex researchers are starting to claim that true bisexuals are few and far between.

And yet, this flies in the face of Kinsey's 1948 report, which asked men to rate their sexual orientation on a scale of 0 to 6, a 6 being exclusively gay. He found 11.6 percent of white men between the ages of twenty and thirty-five scored a 3.

If you want anecdotal evidence, plenty can be found among the famous married, breeding men who get caught up in sex scandals with other men. In 2005 it was then New Jersey governor Jim McGreevey, and in 2007 it was evangelical leader Ted Haggard, both men having made a convincing show of heterosexuality before being outed by male lovers or, in Haggard's case, a male prostitute. Writer Terry McMillan was also briefly married to a man who later revealed he was gay, though he managed to inspire her bestseller *How Stella Got Her Groove Back*. Can a completely gay man revive a woman's groove?

Unfortunately, research in bisexuality is even sparser than that in homosexuality. But around 2005, a few intrepid scientists tried to gather data by wiring up groups of self-reported gay, bisexual, and straight men to a machine that monitored their arousal when they were exposed to erotic images of men and women. The researchers found that, while some of their subjects called themselves bisexual, their male anatomy showed a notable preference for one sex or the other. That led to headlines proclaiming that bisexual men don't exist.

But such a finding would seem to depend on how you define bisexual. Does a person have to be absolutely equally attracted to both sexes? If you like both but slightly prefer one, do you qualify? Scientists don't agree on this. What they do know from tracking the spread of HIV is that a number of men do go both ways. A 2003 survey of HIV-positive men found that 13 percent of white men who reported sex with other men also had sex with women. Among black men it was 34 percent, and among Hispanic men, 26 percent.

"This is something we don't quite understand," said Gerulf Rieger, who headed the 2005 study that reported the nonexistence of bisexuals. Rieger, who is gay, led the study while he was a graduate student in psychology at Northwestern University. When I interviewed him, he said he was baffled by the way so many gay men managed to marry women and pull off a convincing imitation of heterosexuality. In his study, he said he didn't see evidence for "bisexual arousal" among the 101 paid volunteers, recruited using alternative weeklies and gay publications. Of those, 38 identified themselves as gay, 33 as bisexual, and 30 as straight.

To carry out the experiment, he showed the men short films: one with two women having sex, and one with two men having sex. Rieger used the girl-girl sex because previous research already showed that, on average, it was more exciting to heterosexual men than male-female pornography. And heterosexual porn can't distinguish gay from straight men, since gay men are some-times aroused by male-female fare, perhaps focusing on the male partner.

Before the viewing, Rieger and his colleagues hooked their test subjects to their arousal-meter of sorts. "It's quite simple—we put a rubber tube around the penis," said Rieger. "It's filled with mer-cury and that's wired to hardware that goes into a computer."

Nearly a third of the volunteers were rejected from the study because they had no reaction to any of the images. "It makes them very nervous," Rieger said, referring to the experimental apparatus.

For the two-thirds of the men who could handle it, the over-whelming response was always aimed at one sex or the other, even for the self-described bisexuals. And yet, the penis meter did regis-ter a small amount of expansion when most of the straight men watched the other men, and when gays watched the women. Per-haps this tiny bit of bisexuality was what allowed Greek men to so glorify man-boy sex.

But what really surprised Rieger was that some of those men who identified as bisexual responded to the women much more than the men. In that sense they reacted like straight men. Why should a heterosexual man pose as bisexual? "Maybe they're very open," Rieger suggested. "I'm not a straight guy, so I don't know."

An article on the subject in the New York Times appeared under the headline "Straight, Gay or Lying? Bisexuality Revisited." Rieger said the headline came from an expression often bandied about in the gay community and was not meant to imply that bisexual are liars, though that's what it in fact implied. "Some might be truly confused—that's far from being a liar," he said.

Others say it's the scientists who are confused. Lisa Diamond, a professor of psychology and gender identity at the University of Utah, said there's no agreed-upon definition of bisexual, either in science or in society. Some people define their orientation by who they're attracted to, others say it's who you fall in love with that matters. "We have this delusion that we're all talking about the same thing when we talk about arousal and desire and orientation," she said. To dispel the confusion, it might help to put ourselves in the context of the natural world, studying the sometimes slightly more predictable sexual behavior of animals.

HE'S JUST NOT THAT INTO EWE

Critics, pundits, and reporters covered about every conceivable angle involved in the 2005 gay cowboy movie *Brokeback Mountain*, except for the sexual activities of the sheep. As it turns out, the sheep are important, even crucial, in examining one of the most prevalent antigay sentiments of our time—that homosexuality is unnatural.

Beyond the mainstream press, the gay-themed film prompted a flurry of pronouncements on blogs and other electronic forums that homosexual acts go against nature. When such rampant guessing about what is natural or unnatural starts infiltrating cultural debate, it might be time to call in the scientists.

Scientists who spend lots of time watching animals have reported that dozens of creatures, from elk to elephants, climb onto same-sex partners. Killer whales and manatees engage in gay trysts while frolicking in the sea, while gay geese and ducks latch onto one another in devoted male-male or female-female partnerships. And for decades, it turns out, homosexual sheep have been a financial drain on their frustrated breeders. About 8 percent of rams are interested only in other rams, said Charles Roselli, a professor of physiology and pharmacology at Oregon Health and Sciences University.

Roselli tested the sexual orientation of his research rams by penning each one up with sheep of both sexes. He said the gay rams showed no interest in the ewes, but approached other rams and carried out a series of stereotypical mating behaviors. First a gay ram will sniff the genitals of the object of his desire, then do some nuzzling and nibbling, Roselli said. Eventually he will mount the other ram from behind. If it's a same-sex encounter, the mounting ram will ejaculate into its partner's wool. "They don't insert anally," Roselli said. The anatomy isn't quite lined up that way.

When their time arrived to become lamb chops, Roselli took the brains and studied them for gay/straight differences. He found a noticeable difference in part of the brain sometimes called the sexually dimorphic nucleus—a finding he first unveiled at a 2005 scientific meeting of the Endocrine Society, an organization focused on hormone-related research.

That still left open questions about the ram on the bottom. Doesn't putting up with this business suggest he's gay, too? "No one has systematically studied that," Roselli said. But sheep are pretty placid, and may not be bothered by it. While a handful of hypotheses have been advanced to explain gay rams, Roselli said he has long suspected differences in the brain. Humans, like sheep, have a sexually dimorphic nucleus. Located in a brain region called the hypothalamus, this clump of brain cells is bigger in men than in women, and appears to regulate sexual behavior. A study done

in 1991 by neurobiologist Simon LeVay hinted that the sexually dimorphic nucleus also had something to do with sexual orientation,
as it appeared to be about half as large in gay men as in straight
ones. But LeVay was limited to a small sample, and other researchers failed to back up his result.

Critics have contended that gay sheep are the product of
domestication—wild sheep would never do anything like this. But
in his book *Biological Exuberance,* author Bruce Bagemihl details
gay behavior in a huge variety of wild animals. Here's an excerpt
from his section on bighorn mountain rams: "Typically the larger
male rears up on his hind legs and mounts the smaller male. . . .
The mountee assumes a characteristic posture known as lordosis,
in which he arches his back to facilitate copulation. . . . Usually the
mounting male has an erect penis and achieves full anal penetra-
tion." Apparently the anatomy of wild sheep is suited for it. (As is
the anatomy of sheep-herding cowboys, or so they say.)

But the gay sheep don't completely dispel questions from those
in the "homosexuality is unnatural" camp, who often contacted
me while I was writing my newspaper sex column to ask what
evolutionary advantage homosexual behavior might confer. It's
a good question. Some scientists offer that nature thrives on diversity, which gives evolution the raw material it needs. There's
strength in variety, since what may aid survival under some conditions becomes a hindrance in others. This is one of the main points
Joan Roughgarden makes in *Evolution's Rainbow* as she details gay,
lesbian, and transgender behavior all over the tree of life.

She makes the case that gay behavior might have direct advantages in animals that also breed. Social animals, for example,
may thrive if they know what will make them popular not only
with the opposite sex but with everyone. Among captive bonobos,

females practice rampant lesbian sex, rubbing their genitals against each other until they start screeching in ecstasy. A bonobo female who didn't do this might find herself and her offspring social outcasts, unable to acquire and hold the territory or resources they need to survive. The same may go for those mountain rams. They do still mate with ewes on occasion, but they mount other males more, and rams who don't have sex with other rams could find themselves left out of the social order.

Roughgarden paints a more intriguing picture of gay-type behavior in sunfish—a common denizen of North American lakes. Male blue-gilled sunfish come in three distinct forms—a large male, medium male, and small male. The large males are bigger than females, dislike each other, and fight for territory. They are classic alpha males. The small males are classic sneakers—much smaller and ready to dart in and squirt some well-timed sperm in the hope of fertilizing a few eggs.

The medium males are the most mysterious. Slightly smaller than females, they may hang out with them, but nobody knows exactly where they live before breeding season.

When it comes time to breed, the medium males sometimes come into a large male's territory and the two types of males will start going through a series of courtship behaviors, sidling up together and swimming in circles. Other times a female will enter a big male's territory, followed by a medium male. Once cemented in a relationship, the two males and the female mate in a threesome, with the medium male in the middle. The female releases eggs that might meet the sperm of either male.

But the interesting relationship is between the large male and the medium one. Without their courtship and bonding, neither would be as successful in getting a female. Some researchers call the medium males female-mimics and hypothesize that they're fooling the big males into thinking they're females.

Roughgarden disagrees, since she thinks the medium males don't look that much like females and she's not sure that the big males would be that easily fooled. No, she says, the big males are just plain attracted to the medium males for their own qualities, whatever they are.

SHEMALE SNAKES

Beyond bisexuality, homosexuality, and threesomes, human and animal natures offer yet more abundance of sexual variation in the many forms of transgender activity. Cross-dressing is common in humans, and acceptable in women. I can attest that boxer shorts are wonderful to wear, as are men's T-shirts and polo shirts, which are somehow looser and comfier than their counterparts from the women's department. Anything that gets left at my house is fair game. In America at least, this is not considered weird in the least, but if a man puts on women's clothing, he's suddenly labeled a transvestite and his behavior called unnatural.

It's hard to picture transvestite behavior in animals, but snakes do something pretty close, making themselves as convincing as the cross-dressing actor in *The Crying Game*. They don what scientists consider a female perfume—a pheromone that summons other male snakes like sharks to a feeding frenzy.

One snake that shows such gender-bending behavior is the garter snake, which can live as far north as Manitoba—the coldest climate any reptile has dared venture into. In the fall, the snakes find a few deep caves where they hibernate together in a big pile. In spring, the males emerge first, said David Crews, a biologist from the University of Texas, who did much of the groundwork in understanding the pheromone-driven sex lives of snakes.

Then the females emerge one by one or in small groups, where they're mobbed by dozens of males, leading to what's called a "mating ball." Once a female is inseminated, the lucky male leaves her with a "don't cheat on me" pheromone that renders her repulsive to other males.

Crews and others noticed that certain male snakes emitted a female pheromone and thereby attracted a mating ball of other males. "We called these shemales," he said of the male snakes that exuded the male-attracting pheromone. He suspects the shemales aren't gay. They want to mate with females as much as the next guy, but they use their cross-smelling as a tactic to throw off rival males. "It confuses them," Crews said. Biologist Joan Roughgarden doesn't like the term "shemale," which she says is degrading and has been borrowed from the porn industry where it refers to pre-op transsexuals or other transgender women sporting large penises (naughty scientists!).

Scientists sometimes dress male snakes in female scent for experiments. Bob Mason, a snake expert at Oregon State University, did this to isolate the first snake pheromone. He tested different compounds extracted from female snakes by dabbing them on males. Once a scent attracted other males into a mating ball, he knew he'd found it.

You might be tempted to consider this research silly, but there's nothing frivolous about it. In case you missed the campy 2006 hit *Snakes on a Plane*, scientists were the heroes who thwarted the bad guys' attempt to terrorize passengers with pheromone-crazed snakes. That's fiction, you might say, but it's a little-appreciated fact that *Snakes on a Plane* is based on a true story. In the real version, brown tree snakes normally native to Australia or New Guinea stowed away on planes during World War II, invaded Guam, and ate all the songbirds of that once lush island. Today the invasive snake still terrorizes people on Guam and has spread to Hawaii, where it threatens their bird population.

To tackle problems like this we need people like Mason and Crews to understand snakes and their pheromones. You never know when a scientist can be called upon to save humanity from our self-destructive ways.

Mason said he discovered more recently that this transvestite thing wasn't so rare after all. Most male garter snakes do it, but only right after they emerge from hibernation. At that point, they're pretty sluggish, with body temperatures below 40 degrees Fahrenheit, making them easy pickings for birds of prey. But they can warm up faster by putting on some female pheromone, thereby luring other males who've already warmed up a bit to jump on them. These snakes aren't gay then—just cold.

CASES OF SPONTANEOUS SEX CHANGE

In their quest for sex, more than a few animals find ways to act like, look like, or smell like the other sex, or to form intimate relationships with members of their own. For others, if you happen to be losing out as one sex, you can actually switch sides.

"Most fish you see on a coral reef are sex-changing," said Robert Warner, an evolutionary biologist at the University of California. "Groupers, wrasses, parrotfish, damselfish, many of the gobies can change their sex," he said. In some species, when a female achieves a dominant position, she starts to metamorphose into a male. In fish species with a female-dominated hierarchy, a male seizing power will automatically lose his testicles and become the queen. Whichever direction they go, transsexual fish can spontaneously change not only their behavior patterns but their reproductive organs, and often their shape and coloration as well—a mysterious transformation that scientists are only beginning to understand. New research is showing that for us, too, social changes such as marriage and parenthood can alter our sex-hormone levels, but that's about as far as it goes. That's because in humans, sex is set by genetics. With a few exceptions, a gene on the Y chromosome keeps men male for life. But for fish, a combination of genetic and environmental factors can determine sex, making it much more flexible.

And there can be a big evolutionary advantage to changing your sex. Such a trick comes in especially handy in social structures where males dominate groups of many females. Like a sultan with a harem, a dominant male can sire hundreds of offspring while the subordinate males are stuck on the sidelines. In evolution, success means passing down your genes to as many surviving offspring as possible, so if you're a beta male, you're facing possible evolutionary oblivion unless you can improve your rank. If you happen to be a member of a sex-changing species, then you have another option: if you can't beat the guy on top, you can still pass down some genes by joining the harem. You can have a few offspring as a female, and then, if you eventually grow big and tough enough to run the show, you can turn into a male.

In the brilliant orange-and-white clownfish, transsexualism goes the other way. Clownfish groups are headed by a dominant female who rules over a subordinate male and a number of juvenile, asexual fish called satellites. Let's say a fish called Nemo is the biggest of these little asexual fish. If the male died, Nemo could become a male and replace him. If the female died, she'd be replaced by the male. So Nemo could then become a Norma and get to rule the group.

It all starts in the brains of these fish, said Matthew Grober, a biologist from Georgia State University. A change in brain chemistry then initiates a cascade, he said, in which the body is reengineered. Around 2005 he studied this process in the bluebanded goby, a guppy-sized fish that lives along the Southern California coast and in the Sea of Cortez. These gobies cluster in groups of up to ten, each with just one male and a harem of subordinate females. The male keeps the females in line by making threatening approaches, "like a bully in school," Grober said. Males also do a courtship dance that the scientists have called the "jerk swim."

Jerk that he may be, the male keeps everything stable. But if he gets eaten by a bigger fish, as often happens, one of the females will start to change. It's often the biggest of the females that gets to become the new male, but not always, Grober said. The key is dominant behavior. As soon as the male dies or is removed, one female "goes nuts," carrying on a ritualistic bullying of everyone else. That behavior seems to force all her victims to remain female.

Over the next few days, this mean female's body becomes male. The ovaries stop making eggs and turn into testicles. She/he grows a prostate-like gland, and a female appendage she once used to stick eggs into her nest is transformed into a fish version of a penis.

The secret elixir of sex change is an enzyme called aromatase, which turns the male hormone testosterone into estrogen. In females gobies, Grober found, aromatase in the brain keeps them female. But he discovered that levels of this feminizing substance plummeted just as a female starts her sex change. That allowed male hormones to build up and finish the job.

Grober said it's possible that the female, sensing her own newly acquired dominance, starts to act aggressively and that this new behavior is what triggers the physical sex change. This could explain why only one female becomes male. If she starts her aggressive act first, then her behavior simultaneously causes her own masculinization and inhibits it in everyone else. He also found that the process can reverse itself. When he put multiple males together in a tank, one established himself as boss and the others turned female.

The protean nature of fish sex may make them more vulnerable than we humans are to certain pollutants, which often mimic sex hormones. More and more scientists are seeing fish with abnormal sexual development, features of both sexes, as well as groups with too many fish of one sex or the other. In late 2005 a study showed that eleven of eighty-two male fish caught off California had grown ovarian tissues. This does not bode well for the future, especially for males, both human and animal.

And while there's been much joking that women would be better off on our own, perhaps carrying on the human race by cloning ourselves, biology shows we'd run into trouble fast.

14. WHY MALES ARE NECESSARY

NOT FOR SURVIVAL, BUT FOR REPRODUCTION

In her book *Are Men Necessary?* columnist Maureen Dowd detailed numerous gripes with the opposite sex, such as the tendency among certain high achievers to prefer to date secretaries over their professional equals, let alone women above them in the corporate ladder. To back this, she cited a University of Michigan study in which researchers asked undergraduates about their dating and marriage preferences. The young men said that for dating, power didn't matter, but for marriage they'd rather have their secretaries than their bosses because they deemed the secretaries less likely to cheat on them. Dowd lamented another study that purported to show the higher a woman's IQ, the less likely she was to marry. This prompted Dowd to ask, "Do women get less desirable as they get more successful?" IQ isn't synonymous with success by any means, but if the two are correlated at all, the findings could just mean that the higher-IQ women are more capable and therefore better equipped to survive on their own. For certain individual women, men aren't necessary, which shouldn't bother men, and yet it does.

When I asked a variety of men to give me their take on the wide-spread independence of modern women, they said they longed for what they saw as a simpler time of clear-cut roles—a time when every woman needed a man to provide for her and protect her from wild animals. But did such a time ever really exist? Probably not, said James Adovasio, director of the Mercyhurst Archaeological Institute in Erie, Pennsylvania, and one of three authors of the recent book *The Invisible Sex: Uncovering the True Roles of Women in Prehistory*. The popular imagination is still stuck on a quasiscientific narrative called Man the Hunter, which was invented in the late nineteenth and early twentieth centuries, he said. In that scenario, brave male prehumans learned to hunt, the meat they brought back allowing the further growth of the human brain. Women stayed in the caves and begged for meat, offering their sexual favors in exchange for this most precious commodity. In the man-the-hunter world, we all owe our brainpower and our humanity to men. It was a reasonable story, and it made men happy for a long time. But in recent decades, a few uncomfortable observations started to puncture the fantasy.

The fossil record hints that not all meat was hunted. At some hominid sites, animal bones show signs of having been gnawed first by other, fiercer creatures. In other words, our ancestors were scavengers at least some of the time. "How unmanly was that?" said Adovasio. Suddenly modern men were not so eager to get credit for the meat. "Nobody wants to be based on roadkill," he said. Not that men didn't hunt some—but rather than heroically felling mammoths and saber-toothed tigers, they were killing smaller animals and perhaps stealing carcasses from hyenas.

Adovasio said the original glorified picture is no male-chauvinist-pig conspiracy but a natural conclusion that any clever nineteenth-century male scientist would have drawn. From 1830 to 1833, Scottish-born geologist Charles Lyell released three volumes called *Principles of Geology* that vastly expanded humanity's image of our own past, suggesting eons of time before the 6,000-odd-year age of the Earth as calculated using the Bible. Lyell's view not only gave Charles Darwin the time depth he needed to explain his theories of evolution but it allowed people for the first time to contemplate vast stretches of prehistoric human existence known as the Stone Age.

That new understanding led people to start digging up remains from those centuries before cities, farming, or written history. What those early fossil-hunters started to find, said Adovasio, were human skeletons associated with animal bones and stone tools, a juxtaposition that suggested hunting. And it was an automatic conclusion in pre-Victorian society that male domination was an established affair. People of the time also really believed that Stone Age men dragged women around by the hair, said Adovasio. "You can find depictions of the hair-dragging in nineteenth-century art."

PROTECTION RACKET

Adovasio doesn't consider himself a feminist scholar in any official sense. He started thinking about prehistoric sex roles when he began studying the archaeology of relatively perishable items such as textiles, nets, and traps. That turned into a thirty-seven-year career, he said. "When you do that day in and day out, you begin to develop a different view of the past." What he found was a revelation. Imprints of fabrics showed that long before people had advanced beyond basic stone and bone tools, someone was weaving cloth "as fine as a Brooks Brothers shirt." That got him thinking about the people who made it. Were they women or men or both?

Starting in the 1960s and seventies, scholars realized they might gain some additional insights into our preagricultural ancestors by studying the way people live in the few remaining hunter-gatherer groups around the world. In those, he said, men do most of the hunting. But women aren't just sitting around with the babies. They're collecting and processing most of the plants, trapping small game, fishing, making the fish-nets and traps, and sewing most of the clothes, said Adovasio. But men do make most of the shoes, he said. "Why they do that no one knows."

The notion of capable women would have seemed outlandish to the Victorians, Adovasio said. "There was the mythology of frailty and the mythology of emotionalism and the mythology of being hormone-driven. . . . Imagine how dangerous it would be to assume that was no longer the case," he said. "Women would be demanding to vote." Evolutionary psychologist Geoffrey Miller from the University of New Mexico throws even more cold water on the man-the-hunter campfire story in his book *The Mating Mind*. In a hunter-gatherer world where women were capable, men had to compete with other men to impress them, just as they do today. "Men would have tried to show off by hunting game, usually unsuccessfully, returning home empty-handed to beg some yams from the more pragmatic womenfolk," Miller wrote. So in Miller's view, too, this mythical prehistoric time when women universally depended on men much more than men depended on women just didn't happen.

While other evolutionary psychologists point to a universal female preference for high-status, strong, intelligent, and rich men, Miller said we shouldn't assume that women always loved men for their money, or that our ancestors were gold diggers. In the past, before male land ownership and patriarchy gave men so much power, women could go out and get their own food. In some of the Native American groups that had developed farming, the women tended the fields and owned the land, giving them independence and power to choose their mates—or divorce them. So those universal preferences for successful men might have had more to do with those traits that signaled good genes, Miller said. Women in the past who liked those traits were more likely to produce children with those traits—and those children were more likely to propagate their mothers' genes.

Taking men one last step off their pedestal, Miller wrote that most predators were either strong enough to kill a man or woman with equal ease or were weak enough that either sex could fight them off. Men weren't necessary to protect women from predators. Of course what men traditionally did protect women from was other men, as now-retired University of California anthropologist Sarah Blaffer Hrdy pointed out in her 1999 book *Mother Nature*. She called it a protection racket.

How do the men helping to create this new, less male-centric, story of humanity feel about it? Are they diminished by the loss of their man-the-hunter story? "I may be a special case," said Adovasio. He was raised by a single mother after his father died in World War II. She was a multiple major in college and a star athlete who competed in several different sports. As a woman physically gifted in strength and speed, he said, "My mother could take out most males I'd ever known." That's given him a different perspective, he said, in that he never had to feel superior to women. And let's not forget that if our prehistoric ancestors couldn't impress women with their hunting skills, they still had another ace in the hole. If they were anything like foraging groups today, the men made most of the shoes, said Adovasio. "The early Prada folks were men." What could be more necessary than that?

Some men get nervous about the prospect of cloning. Should they be? Could that render them unnecessary, even for sex? In a handful of other species, males have gotten phased out after females developed the ability to give birth without them. It's happened in the whiptail lizards of the American Southwest, for example. But as a general rule species don't last long once they lose their males, said biologist Ricardo Azevedo of the University of Houston, an expert on the importance of sex in the natural world. Most all-girl species cropped up relatively recently, he said, because in the long haul, most species need males to stave off genetic degradation.

Biologists have found that males are necessary even in some species where the females acquired the ability to make their own sperm—thus qualifying as hermaphrodites. This happens occasionally in nature, since hermaphroditism has its advantages. If you want to colonize new ponds or tide pools, it can help to be able to mate with anyone of your species, including—in a pinch—yourself. It works well for some corals, barnacles, shellfish, worms, and many plants.

If the females are the ones that turn into hermaphrodites, it would seem to put the remaining males in a desperate position, and yet that's more or less what happened to the male clam shrimp, a puddle and pond dweller that thrives on all continents except Antarctica. Millions of years ago a mutant female started producing both sperm and eggs. That mutation, or series of mutations, spread until all the females were replaced by hermaphrodites. Females also acquired the ability to make sperm in one of our fellow vertebrates, a swamp dweller called a killifish. And yet male killifish keep cropping up here and there, though you'd think a hermaphrodite fish would need a male about as much as it needs, well, a bicycle.

"In some ways it is a matter of 'jack of all trades is a master of none,'" said Stephen Weeks, an evolutionary ecologist from the University of Akron, Ohio. The hermaphroditic clam shrimp he studies, for example, can't mate with other hermaphrodites of their species. Only the males come equipped with a clawlike clasper, necessary for holding another clam shrimp in the proper position for its eggs to meet his sperm at the right time. In the absence of males, the hermaphrodite shrimp are stuck mating with themselves, said Weeks, and that's a problem. "That's often associated with something called inbreeding depression, which is, basically . . . have you seen *Deliverance?*"

You can't get more incestuous than sex with yourself. It's not cloning—you're not making a genetic copy of yourself. To make eggs and sperm, a hermaphrodite divides its genes in half in many different ways, then brings the two halves back together. That process will often double up copies of any deleterious genes you happen to carry. Say you're a hermaphrodite and you carry a recessive gene for banjo savant syndrome, or BSS. You're normal, since you need two copies of the mutant BSS gene to have the disease and your cells carry just one BSS copy, plus a normal copy. But you divide your genes in half to make sperm, so half your sperm get a mutant copy of the BSS gene. The same thing happens in your eggs. That means one of every four of your offspring will get two mutant BSS genes and come out banjo savants. And if they're fertile, *all* their offspring will be banjo savants.

Preventing this kind of thing is the job of the male clam shrimp, and apparently has been for some time. All of the more than thirty known species of this creature mix hermaphrodites and males, which suggests that they inherited this mating system from a common ancestor before they diverged, which the fossil record says happened more than 24 million years ago. Genetic diversity also keeps the male killifish in business despite the challenge of having to mate with hermaphrodites—and mean ones at that. When you put killifish together in a tank, the hermaphrodites tend to eat the males, said biologist John Elder of Valdosta State University in Georgia. The hermaphrodites are also too mean to mate with each other and live to tell about it. As a general rule when they meet, they "go after each other like piranhas," said Elder. In captivity they never have sex with other fish, thus depending on self-fertilization to reproduce.

And yet in the wild, some males obviously mate and escape, at least in Belize, where DNA tests show that males inject much-needed genetic diversity into the pool. For years, the scientists weren't finding any males among Florida's killifish, but genetic tests later showed the Floridian fish are much too genetically diverse to be having sex just with themselves. It seems likely that males not yet spotted are mixing up the genes, bravely having sex with the vicious hermaphrodites. These males seem to be fighting against all odds, but the quest for sex keeps them in the game.

CONCLUSION

WHO WE ARE

Males may not be absolutely necessary to the propagation of life, but without them life wouldn't have gotten interesting. Males and females were both necessary for sex to propel the living world toward the vast and colorful diversity of species we see. Sex and the competition for sex made us who we are. But who are we? Where has all that sex-propelled evolution left us?

Some argue that eons of competition for sex endowed us with creativity, generosity, and intelligence far beyond what we need for survival alone. Others would say sex made us warlike. In our species and others, males fight for power and use that power to get sex. The expression "make love not war" should probably be amended to "make love without war," or maybe, "make music not war." At the bottom of it all, making love is the ultimate reward for the winners in war, as it is for the winners in almost everything else.

Not all creatures go after sex in the same way. Some by nature desire nothing more than to bond with one single mate and devote themselves to parenting. Others want to experience as many mates as possible, oblivious to any offspring that result. Some bring force and brawn to the field of competition and some bring beauty. What is the natural mating strategy for human beings? The old cliché that men want to get around and women to settle down doesn't quite square with real life. Even in cultures without strict rules about marriage, men often bond with women for periods of years, helping them raise children. Some men are monogamous by nature, some promiscuous, and some switch from one way of life to the other as they mature. Women show the same flexibility, able to adopt different mating strategies depending on the surrounding culture and their personal best interests. We may pine for some universal ideal or rule governing our sex lives but it doesn't exist. As biologist Robert Sapolsky put it, "We're one confused species."

We also tend to get confused between mate value, as the evolutionary psychologists call it, and value as human beings. Are beautiful women better people? Are they more worthy of life? Are handsome, gregarious, charming men more valuable to society? We often respond to them as if they are, but somehow we know they aren't.

Pickup artists take the philosophical position that mate value matters but you don't have to accept what nature hands you. Self-improvement is part of the game of sex as human beings play it.

When the pickup boot camp ended, the instructor, Future, walked me back to the train station. He teased and joked that if he really went full throttle with his technique he could convince me to cheat on my boyfriend. I teased back, knowing that was impossible. But before I said goodbye, I asked him what he really wanted in life. He told me that since he became equipped with the right social skills, he now does exactly what he wants, which is to rotate through a whole merry-go-round of women and add the occasional new one when the opportunity arises. He admitted that the women in his sex circle were probably sleeping with other men, too. If there weren't women eager to break from the monogamous life, men like Future wouldn't have much luck.

To me, his sex life sounded like a full-time job. Why go through so much effort, I asked him. He saw his so-called polyamorous life-style as easier than monogamy. I saw it the other way around. Luckily, as I've come to realize, some men are monogamous by nature, or at least they develop the capacity for it when they reach a certain age. And I had one of those waiting for me at home.

SOURCES AND REFERENCES

1. THE MYSTERY

Strauss, Neil. *The Game: Penetrating the Secret Society of Pickup Artists* (William Morrow, 2005). Details the adventures of the author as he learns the art of picking up women and incorporates himself into so-called pickup culture. There's much interesting insight into the way some men think and tips anyone might use to win friends and influence people in the post–Dale Carnegie era.

Mystery. *The Mystery Method: How to Get Beautiful Women Into Bed* (St. Martin's Press, 2007). A more nuts-and-bolts guide for men who want to learn "the Method." There's still news anyone can use, as well as a glimpse into "Mystery's" mind, for those so inclined to look.

Sapolsky, R. *Monkeyluv: And Other Essays on Our Lives as Animals* (Scribner, 2005).

SCHOLARLY REFERENCES FOR EXPERIMENTS IN MATE COPYING AND PLAYING HARD-TO-GET:

Dugatkin, L. "Sexual Selection and Imitation: Females Copy the Mate Choice of Others," *American Naturalist* 139(6):1384–1389 (1992).

Fiorillo, C., P. Tobler, and W. Schultz. "Discrete Codling of Reward Probability and Uncertainty by Dopamine Neurons," *Science* 299:1898–1902 (2003).

Eastwick, P., et al. "Selective Versus Unselective Romantic Desire: Not all Reciprocity Is Created Equal," *Psychological Science* 18(4):317–319 (Oct. 2007).

2. LET THERE BE SEXES

FOR MORE ON THE ORIGIN AND EARLY HISTORY OF LIFE:

Mojzsis, S. J. "Origin of Life: The First Fossils," in *Encyclopedia of Evolution,* edited by M. Pagel (Oxford University Press, 2002).

Mojzsis, S. J., and T. M. Harrison. "Establishment of a 3.83 Ga Magmatic Age for the Akilia Tonalite (Southern West Greenland)," *Earth and Planetary Science Letters* 202:563–576 (2002).

———. "Origin and Significance of Archean Quartzose Rocks at Akilia, Greenland," *Science* 298:917a (2002).

Anbar, A. D., et al. "Extraterrestrial Iridium, Sediment Accumulation and the Habitability of the Early Earth's Surface," *Journal of Geophysical Research* 106(2):3219–3236 (2001).

Mojzsis, S. J. "Life and the Evolution of Earth's Atmosphere," in *Earth—Inside and Out,* edited by E. Mathez (New Press, 2001).

Mojzsis, S. J., and T. M. Harrison. "Vestiges of a Beginning: Clues to the Emergent Biosphere Recorded in the Oldest Known Sedimentary Rocks," *GSA Today* 10:1–6 (2000).

"THE PARASITIC SEX?" FOR MORE ON THIS VIEW OF THE ORIGIN OF THE MALE AND FEMALE SEXES:

Parker, G. A., R. R. Baker, and V.G.F. Smith. "The Origin and Evolution of Gamete Dimorphism and the Male-Female Phenomenon," *Journal of Theoretical Biology* 36:529–533 (1972).

Matsuda, H., and P. Abrams. "Why Are Equally Sized Gametes So Rare? The Instability of Isogamy and the Cost of Anisogamy," *Evolutionary Ecology Research* 1:769–784 (1999).

Lessels, C. M., R. R. Snook, and D. J. Hosken. "The Evolutionary Origin and Maintenance of Sperm: Selection for a Small, Motile Gamete Mating Type," *Sperm Evolution* (in press at time of publication).

Bjork, A., and S. Pitnick. "Intensity of Sexual Selection Along the Anisogamy-Isogamy Continuum," *Nature* (letter), 441(7094):742–745 (June 8, 2006).

"THE CLEANER SEX?" FOR MORE ON THIS ALTERNATIVE VIEW OF THE SEXES:

Hurst, L. "Parasite Diversity and the Evolution of Diploidy, Multicellularity and Anisogamy," *Journal of Theoretical Biology* 144:429–443 (1990).

Hurst, L., and W. Hamilton. "Cytoplasmic Fusion and the Nature of the Sexes," *Proceedings of the Royal Society* B 247:189–194 (1992).

Hurst, L. "Selfish Genetic Elements and Their Role in Evolution: The Evolution of Sex and Some of What That Entails," *Philosophical Transactions of the Royal Society of London* B 349:321–332 (1995).

———. "Why Are There Only Two Sexes?" *Proceedings: Biological Sciences* 263(1369):415–422 (1996).

Randerson, J., and L. Hurst. "The Uncertain Evolution of the Sexes," *Trends in Ecology and Evolution* 10:571–579 (2001).

AND FOR THE GROUNDBREAKING WORK OF LYNN MARGULIS:

Margulis, Lynn. *Early Life* (Science Books International, 1982).

———. *Origin of Eukaryotic Cells* (Yale University Press, 1970).

3. COMPETING FOR FEMALES

HITCHENS'S DEFENSE OF HIS POLITICALLY INCORRECT THESIS:

Hitchens, Christopher. "Why Women Aren't Funny," *Vanity Fair* (Jan. 2007).

THE STANFORD STUDY TO WHICH HITCHENS REFERS:

Eiman, A., et al. "Sex Differences in Brain Activation Elicited by Humor," *Proceedings of the National Academy of Sciences* 102(45):16496–16501 (2005).

SOME BOOKS I FOUND USEFUL FOR EXPLAINING BASIC SEX DIFFERENCES:

Bribiescas, Richard. *Men: Evolutionary and Life History* (Harvard University Press, 2006). A scholarly look at the evolution of men that explains how our current male/female differences evolved from our apelike ancestors.

Majerus, Michael. *Sex Wars: Genes, Bacteria, and Biased Sex Ratios* (Princeton University Press, 2003). From feminizing bacteria to male-killing invaders, the surprising natural phenomena covered in this scholarly book explain the evolution of sex, sex differences, and various ways of determining sex, as well as a host of special risks to males, especially in the insect world.

**FOR MORE INFORMATION ON BROADCAST SPAWNING AND
THE EVOLUTION OF SEX DIFFERENCES:**

Levitan, D. R. "Relationship Between Egg Size and Fertilization Success in Broadcast Spawning Invertebrates," *Integrative and Comparative Biology* 46:298–311 (2006).

———. "The Distribution of Male and Female Reproductive Success in a Broadcast Spawning Invertebrate," *Integrative and Comparative Biology* 4:848–855 (2005).

Levitan, D. R., and D. L. Ferrell. "Selection on Gamete Recognition Proteins Depends on Sex Genotype Frequency," *Science* 312:267–269 (2006).

FURTHER EVIDENCE THAT MEN TRY HARDER:

Kruger, D. J., and R. M. Nesse. "Sexual Selection and the Male:Female Mortality Ratio," *Evolutionary Psychology* 2:66–77 (2004).

4. SEX DRIVE

Leonardi, Tommy. *The Secrets of Sensual Lovemaking: How to Give Her the Ultimate Pleasure* (Dutton Adult, 1995). I never read it but I spoke with the author and he told me all I need to know.

Soble, Alan. *The Philosophy of Sex and Love: An Introduction* (Paragon House Publishers, 1998). Like all of Soble's books, this offers many thought-provoking essays that could change the way you look at sex.

Seawell, Joan. *I'd Rather Eat Chocolate: Learning to Love My Low Libido* (Broadway Books, 2007).

FOR MORE ON THE BATTLE OF THE SEXES IN HERMAPHRODITES:

Anthes, N., A. Putz, and N. Michiels. "Hermaphrodite Sex Role Preferences: The Role of Partner Body Size, Mating History and Female Fitness in the Sea Slug Chelidonura Sandrana," *Behavioral Ecology and Sociobiology* 60:359–367 (2006).

———. "Sex Role Preferences, Gender Conflict and Sperm Trading in Simultaneous Hermaphrodites: A New Framework," *Animal Behavior* 72: 1–12 (2006).

———. "Gender Trading in a Hermaphrodite," *Current Biology* 15:R792–R793 (Oct. 11, 2005).

Charnov, E. L. "Simultaneous Hermaphroditism and Sexual Selection," *Proceedings of the National Academy of Sciences* 76:2480–2484 (May 1, 1979).

Michiels, N. K., and L. J. Newman. "Sex and Violence in Hermaphrodites," *Nature* 391:647 (Feb. 12, 1998).

Milius, Susan. "Battle of the Hermaphrodites," *Science News* 170(12):186 (2006).

———. "Hermaphrodites Duel for Manhood," *Science News* 153(5): 101–102 (Feb. 14, 1998).

Soble, Alan. *Sexual Investigations* (New York University Press, 1997). I found this the most accessible of his books on the philosophy of sex. Soble takes a scholarly look at guilt, pleasure, love, power, bondage, and more.

FOR MORE ON THE USE OF EXPLICIT FILMS IN RESEARCH:

Binik, I., and T. Kukkonen. Canadian Sex Research Forum, Ottowa (Sept. 2006).

5. THE GENETICS OF MEN

Sykes, Bryan. *Adam's Curse: The Science That Reveals Our Genetic Destiny* (W.W. Norton & Company, 2005). This book goes into great detail about the origin and fate of our sex chromosomes and has some gloomy things to say about males in general.

**SCHOLARLY REFERENCES ON VARIOUS WAYS TO DETERMINE SEX,
SUCH AS TEMPERATURE:**

Spotila, J., et al. "Hot and Cold Running Dinosaurs: Body Size, Metabolism and Migration," *Modern Geology* 16:203–227 (1991).

Lance, V. "Introduction: Environmental Sex Determination in Reptiles: Patterns and Processes," *Journal of Experimental Zoology* 270:1–2 (1994).

Spotila, L., J. Spotila, and N. Kaufer. "Molecular Mechanisms of TSD in Reptiles: A Search for the Magic Bullet." *Journal of Experimental Zoology* 270:117–127 (1994).

Wibbels, T., J. Bull, and D. Crews. "Temperature-Dependant Sex Determination: A Mechanistic Approach," *Journal of Experimental Zoology* 270:71–79 (1994).

Paladino, F., J. Spotila, and P. Dodson. "A Blueprint For Giants: Modeling the Physiology of Large Dinosaurs," chapter 34 in Farlow and Brett-Surman, eds., *The Complete Dinosaur* (Indiana University Press, 1997).

SCHOLARLY REFERENCES ON THE DISCOVERY OF THE MALE-MAKING GENE:

Koopman, P., et al. "Male Development of Chromosomally Female Mice Transgenic for SRY," *Nature* 1351:117–121 (1991).

Morais da Silva, S., et al. "SOX9 Expression During Gonadal Development Implies a Conserved Role for Gene in Testis Differentiation in Mammals and Birds," *Nature Genetics* 14:62–68 (1996).

OTHER ROLES FOR SRY IN THE BRAIN:

Dewing. P., et al. "Direct Regulation of Adult Brain Function by the Male-Specific Factor SRY," *Current Biology* 16(4):415–420 (2006).

SCHOLARLY REFERENCES ON HUMANS WITH REVERSED SEX CHROMOSOMES:

Parma, P., et al. "R-spondin1 is Essential in Sex Determination, Skin Differentiation, and Malignancy," *Nature Genetics*, advance online publications, 38:1304–1309 (Oct. 15, 2006).

Wilhelm, D. "R-spondin1-Discovery of the Long-Missing, Mammalian Female-Determining Gene?" *BioEssays* 29:314–318 (2007).

FOR MORE ON THE SCIENCE OF JESUS:

Tipler, Frank. *The Physics of Christianity* (Doubleday, 2007).

SCHOLARLY REFERENCES ON THE ORIGIN AND POSSIBLE DISAPPEARANCE OF THE Y CHROMOSOME:

Marshall Graves, J. "From Brain Determination to Testis Determination: Evolution of the Mammalian Sex-Determining Gene," *Reproduction, Fertility and Development* 13:665–672 (2001).

———. "Sex and Death in Birds: A Model of Dosage Compensation That Predicts Lethality of Sex Chromosome Aneuploids," *Cytogenetic and Genome Research* 101:278–282 (2003).

————. "Recycling the Y Chromosome," *Science,* Perspectives, 378:50–51 (Jan. 7, 2005).

Marshall Graves, J., and S. Shetty. "Sex From W to Z: Evolution of Vertebrate Sex Chromosomes and Sex Determining Genes," *Journal of Experimental Zoology* 290:449–462 (2001).

REFERENCES ON THE PLATYPUS SEX CHROMOSOMES AND WHAT THEY TELL US ABOUT MEN:

Khamsi, R. "Duck-Billed Platypus Boasts Ten Sex Chromosomes," *Nature* (Oct. 25, 2004).

Marshall Graves, J. "Sex Chromosome Specialization and Degeneration in Mammals," *Cell* 124 (March 10, 2006).

Rens, W., et al. "Resolution and Evolution of the Duck-Billed Platypus Karyotype with an $X_1Y_1X_2Y_2X_3Y_3X_4Y_4X_5Y_5$ Male Sex Chromosome Constitution," *Proceedings of the National Academy of Science* 101(46):16257–16261 (Nov. 16, 2004); published online Nov. 8, 2004.

AND FOR THE MORE OPTIMISTIC VIEW OF THE FUTURE OF THE Y:

Hughes, J., et al. "Conservation of Y-Linked Genes During Human Evolution Revealed by Comparative Sequencing in Chimpanzee," *Nature* 436 (7055):101–104 (2005).

Cordum, H., et al. "The Male-Specific Region of the Human Y Chromosome Is a Mosaic of Discrete Sequence Classes," *Nature* 423:825–837 (2003).

Rozen, S., et al. "Abundant Gene Conversion between Arms of Palindromes in Human and Ape Y Chromosomes," *Nature* 423:873–876 (2003).

6. PRIVATE PARTS

Friedman, David. *A Mind of Its Own* (Free Press, 2001). A surprisingly erudite and enlightening book on the cultural history of the penis from ancient Greece to Freud to feminism.

A PAPER DR. KELLY SENT ME ABOUT HER WORK ON PHALLOLOGY:

Kelly, D. "The Functional Morphology of Penile Erection: Tissue Designs for Increasing and Maintaining Stiffness," *Integrative and Comparative Biology* 42:216–221 (2002).

FOR THE ORIGINAL PAPER ON SEX IN THE MRI TUBE:

Schultz, W., et al. "Magnetic Resonance Imaging of Male and Female Genitals During Coitus and Female Sexual Arousal," *British Medical Journal* 319:1596–1600 (1999).

FOR MORE IN THE HISTORY OF PHALLOLOGY:

Clark, K., and C. Pedreti. *The Drawings of Leonardo da Vinci in the Collection of Her Majesty the Queen at Windsor Castle* (Phaidon, 1968).

WITH REGARD TO PENIS SIZE:

Studies that rely on self-reporting suffer from an obvious bias, but in the mid-1990s researchers used a drug to induce erections in eighty men who measured the length themselves. The researchers got an average length of 5.08 inches, which they published in the *Journal of Urology*.

Wessells, H., T. Lue, and J. McAninch. "Penile Length in the Flaccid and Erect States: Guidelines for Penile Augmentation," *Journal of Urology* 156(3): 995–997 (1996).

Sparling, Joseph. "Penile Erections: Shape, Angle, and Length," *Journal of Sex & Marital Therapy* 23(3):195–207 (1997).

da Ros, C., et al. "Caucasian Penis: "What Is the Normal Size?" *Journal of Urology*, part 2, 151:323A (1994). Other somewhat similar studies got averages of 5.35 inches and then 5.0. That last number was from a study sponsored by Lifestyle Condoms that relied on college students during a spring break in Cancun.

Judson, Olivia. *Dr. Tatiana's Sex Advice to All Creation* (Vintage, 2003). A delightful book on the strange sex lives of our fellow creatures, all composed as a faux sex-advice column.

SCHOLARLY REFERENCES ON SPERM-COMPETITION THEORY AND HOW THIS MIGHT INFLUENCE EVOLUTION OF THE HUMAN PENIS AND THE HUMAN STYLE OF SEX:

Baker, R., and M. Bellis. "Human Sperm Competition: Ejaculate Adjustment by Males and the Function of Masturbation," *Animal Behaviour* 46:861–885 (1993).

———. "Human Sperm Competition: Ejaculate Manipulation by Females and a Function for the Female Orgasm," *Animal Behaviour* 46:887–909 (1993).

Bellis, M., and R. Baker. "Do Females Promote Sperm Competition: Data for Humans," *Animal Behaviour* 40:997–999 (1990).

Shackelford, T., N. Pound, and A. Goetz. "Psychological and Physiological Adaptations to Sperm Competition in Humans," *Review of General Psychology* 9:228–248 (2005).

Goetz, A., and T. Shackelford. "Sperm Competition Theory Offers Additional Insight into Cultural Variation in Sexual Behavior," *Behavioral and Brain Sciences* 28:285–286 (2005).

Shackelford, T., and A. Goetz. "Comparative Evolutionary Psychology of Sperm Competition," *Journal of Comparative Psychology* 120:139–146 (2006).

———. "Adaptation to Sperm Competition in Humans," *Current Directions in Psychological Science* 16:47–50 (2007).

Shackelford, T., et al. "Absence Makes the Adaptations Grow Fonder: Proportion of Time Apart from Partner, Male Sexual Psychology, and Sperm Competition in Humans (Homo sapiens)," *Journal of Comparative Psychology* 121:214–220 (2007).

Starratt, V., et al. "Male Mate Retention Behaviors Vary with Risk of Female Infidelity and Sperm Competition," *Acta Psychologica Sinica* 39:523–527 (2007).

ORIGINAL PAPER ON DUCK PENIS/VAGINA COEVOLUTION:

Brennan, P., et al. "Coevolution of Male and Female Genital Morphology in Waterfowl," *Public Library of Science ONE* 2(5), (2007).

MORE ON THE G-SPOT AND THE HOMOLOGY BETWEEN
MALE AND FEMALE SEX ORGANS:

Addiego, F., et al. "Female Ejaculation: A Case Study," *The Journal of Sex Research* 17:13–21 (1981).

———. "Female Ejaculation," *Medical Aspects of Human Sexuality* 14:99–100 (1980).

Belzer, E., B. Whipple, and W. Moger. "On Female Ejaculation," *The Journal of Sex Research* 20:403–406 (1984).

Bullough, B., et al. "Subjective Reports of Female Orgasmic Expulsion of Fluid," *The Nurse Practitioner* 9:55–59 (1984).

Goldberg, D., et al. "The Grafenberg Spot and Female Ejaculation: A Review of Initial Hypotheses," *Journal of Sex and Marital Therapy* 9:27–37 (1983).

Whipple, Beverly, John Perry, and Alice Kahn Ladas. *The G Spot: And Other Discoveries about Human Sexuality* (Owl Books, 2004).

7. TESTOSTERONE

GENERAL REFERENCES:

Jones, Steve. *Y: The Descent of Men* (Houghton-Mifflin, 2003).

Fisher, Helen. *Anatomy of Love: The Natural History of Monogamy, Adultery and Divorce* (W.W. Norton & Company, 1992).

FOR THE ORIGINAL SOURCES ON TESTOSTERONE
AND "TESTOSTERONE POISONING":

Alda, Alan. "What Every Woman Should Know about Men," *Ms.* (Oct. 1975).

Sullivan, Andrew. "The He Hormone," *New York Times Magazine* (April 2, 2000).

Roughgarden, Joan. *Evolution's Rainbow* (University of California Press, 2004).

SCHOLARLY REFERENCES ON THE EFFECTS OF TESTOSTERONE
ON MEN'S PHYSIOLOGY, HEALTH, AND BEHAVIOR:

Booth, A., and J. Dabbs. "Testosterone and Men's Marriages," *Social Forces* 72:463–477 (1993).

Laughlin, G., and E. Barrett-Connor. "Testosterone Deficiency May Increase Risk of Death in Older Men." Talk at the Endocrine Society's Annual Meeting (June 2007).

Bateup, H., et al. "Testosterone, Cortisol, and Women's Competition," *Evolution and Human Behavior* 23:181–192 (2002).

McIntyre, M., et al. "Romantic Involvement Often Reduces Men's Testosterone Levels—But Not Always: The Moderating Roles of Extra-Pair Sexual Interest," *Journal of Personality and Social Psychology* 91:642–651 (2006).

Gray, P., C. Yang, and H. Pope, Jr. "Fathers Have Lower Salivary Testosterone Levels Than Unmarried Men and Married Non-Fathers in Beijing, China," *Proceedings of the Royal Society of London* B 273:333–339 (2006).

Gray, P. "Marriage, Parenting and Testosterone Variation Among Kenyan Swahili Men," *American Journal of Physical Anthropology* 122:279–286 (2003).

Burnham, T., et al. "Men in Committed, Romantic Relationships Have Lower Testosterone Than Single Men," *Hormones and Behavior* 44:119–122 (2003).

Gray, P., et al. "Marriage and Fatherhood Are Associated with Lower Testosterone in Males," *Evolution and Human Behavior* 23:193–201 (2002).

SCHOLARLY REFERENCE ON FINGER LENGTH AND SEX:

Salmon, C., and D. Symons. "Slash Fiction and Human Mating Psychology," *Journal of Sex Research* 41 (Feb. 2004).

SOME GOOD REFERENCES ON GENETIC DISORDERS THAT INTERFERE WITH TESTOSTERONE AND SEXUAL DEVELOPMENT:

Imperato-McGinley, J., et al. "Steroid 5α-Reductase Deficiency in Man: An Inherited Form of Male Pseudohermaphroditism," *Science* 186(4170): 1213–1215 (Dec. 27, 1974).

Imperato-McGinley, J., et al. "Androgens and the Evolution of Male-Gender Identity Among Male Pseudohermaphrodites with 5-Alpha-Reductase Deficiency," *New England Journal of Medicine* 300:1233–1237 (1979).

Herdt, G. "Mistaken Gender: 5-Alpha Reductase Hermaphroditism and Biological Reductionism in Sexual Identity Reconsidered," *American Anthropologist*, n.s., 92(2):443–446 (June 1990).

MORE BOOKS OF INTEREST ON GENDER AND HORMONES:

Colapinto, John. *As Nature Made Him: The Boy Who Was Raised As a Girl* (Harper Collins, 2000). This fascinating book offers a journalistic account of a tragic tale. Medical arrogance leads a top sex researcher to believe he can transform a boy damaged by a botched circumcision into a girl. He couldn't.

Eugenides, Jeffrey. *Middlesex* (Farrar, Straus and Giroux, 2002).

Valerio, Max Wolf. *The Testosterone Files: My Hormonal and Social Transformation from Female to Male* (Seal Press, 2006). The personal memoir of a woman who became a man.

8. THE SECRET LIVES OF SPERM

SOME REFERENCES ON THE HISTORY OF OUR UNDERSTANDING OF SPERM AND HUMAN REPRODUCTION IN GENERAL:

Silver, Lee. *Challenging Nature: The Clash of Science and Spirituality at the New Frontiers of Life* (Ecco, 2006).

Friedman, David. *A Mind of Its Own* (Free Press, 2001).

SCHOLARLY REFERENCES ON CONTEMPORARY SPERM-RELATED SCIENCE:

Dorus, S., et al. "Towards a Drosophila Sperm Proteome: A Whole-Cell Analysis of Function and Evolution," *Nature Genetics* (Advanced Online Publication, 2006).

Immler, S., et al. "By Hook or by Crook? Morphometry, Competition and Cooperation in Rodent Sperm," *Public Library of Science ONE* 2(1):e170 (2007).

SCHOLARLY REFERENCES ON SPERM COMPETITION AND THE EVOLUTION OF MALE SEXUALITY:

Baker, R., and M. Bellis. "Number of Sperm in Human Ejaculates Varies in Accordance with Sperm Competition Theory," *Animal Behaviour* 37: 867–869 (1989).

———. "Elaboration of the 'Kamikaze' Sperm Hypothesis: A Reply to Harcourt," *Animal Behaviour* 37:865–867 (1989).

———. "'Kamikaze' Sperm in Mammals?" *Animal Behaviour* 36:937–980 (1988).

———. "Human Sperm Competition: Ejaculate Adjustment by Males and the Function of Masturbation," *Animal Behaviour* 46:861–885 (1993).

Gallup, G., and R. Burch. "Semen Displacement as a Sperm Competition Strategy in Humans," *Evolutionary Psychology* 4:12–23 (2004).

Gallup, G., et al. "The Human Penis As a Semen Displacement Device," *Evolution and Human Behavior* 24:277–289 (2003).

Goetz, A., et al. "Mate Retention, Semen Displacement, and Human Sperm Competition: A Preliminary Investigation of Tactics to Prevent and Correct Female Infidelity," *Personality and Individual Differences* 38:749–763 (2005).

Shackelford, T., et al. "Psychological Adaptation to Human Sperm Competition," *Evolution and Human Behavior* 23:123–138 (2002).

Shackelford, T., and A. Goetz. "Comparative Psychology of Sperm Competition," *Journal of Comparative Psychology* 120:139–146 (2006).

Shackelford, T., N. Pound, and A. Goetz. "Psychological and Physiological Adaptations to Sperm Competition in Humans," *Review of General Psychology* 9:228–248 (2005).

Platek, S., and T. Shackelford. *Female Infidelity and Paternal Uncertainty* (Kindle Books, 2007).

9. ARE MEN SCUM?

Pinker, Steven. *How the Mind Works* (W.W. Norton & Company, 1997). This book may not really explain how the mind works but it's still a fascinating tour through evolutionary psychology, with a whole chapter devoted to sexuality.

FOR MORE ON DAVID BUSS'S WORK EXPLAINING SEX DIFFERENCES IN SEXUAL BEHAVIOR:

Buss, D. M. "Sex Differences in Human Mate Preferences: Evolutionary Hypotheses Tested in 37 Cultures," *Behavioral and Brain Sciences* 12:1–49 (1989).

————."Psychological Sex Differences: Origins Through Sexual Selection," *American Psychologist* 50:164–168 (1995).

————. "Paternity Uncertainty and the Complex Repertoire of Human Mating Strategies," *American Psychologist* 51(2): 161–162 (1996).

Buss, D. M., and D. P. Schmitt. "Strategic Self-Promotion and Competition Derogation: Sex and Conflict Effects on Perceived Effectiveness of Mate Attraction Tactics," *Journal of Personality and Social Psychology* 70(6):1185–1204 (1996).

Buss, D. M., R. J. Larsen, and D. Westin. "Sex Differences in Jealousy: Not Gone, Not Forgotten, and Not Explained by Alternative Hypotheses," *Psychological Science* 7(6): 373–375 (1996).

Buss, D. M., et al. "International Preferences in Selecting Mates: A Study of 37 Societies," *Journal of Cross-Cultural Psychology* 21:5–47 (1990).

Buunk, B. P., et al. "Sex Differences in Jealousy in Evolutionary and Cultural Perspective: Tests from the Netherlands, Germany, and the United States," *Psychological Science* 7(6): 359–363 (1996).

OTHER SOURCES FOR THIS CHAPTER:

Geraci, Ron. *The Bachelor Chronicles* (Kensington, 2006). Offers all sorts of information some women might want to know about picky single guys in New York.

Longman, P. "The Return of Patriarchy," *Foreign Policy* 56–65 (March/April 2006).

Sandborn, Calvin. *Becoming the Kind Father* (New Society Publishers, 2007). A personal memoir that chronicles one man's discovery of his long-lost feminine side.

Buss, David. *The Murderer Next Door: Why the Mind Is Designed to Kill* (Penguin Press, 2005).

"She Still Belonged to Him"—From interviews conducted by the United Nations Population Fund for its report "The Dynamics of Honor Killings in Turkey," *Harper's* 24 (Sept. 2007).

FOR MORE ON GRANNY FETISHES AMONG CHIMPANZEES:

Muller, M. N., M. Emery Thompson, and R. W. Wrangham. "Male Chimpanzees Prefer Mating with Old Females," *Current Biology* 16:2234–2238 (2006).

10. BEAUTY AND BEASTS

SCHOLARLY REFERENCES ON PEAHEN PREFERENCES IN PEACOCKS:

Loyau, A., et al. "Male Sexual Attractiveness Affects Investment of Maternal Resources into the Eggs in Peafowl (*Pavo cristatus*)," *Behavioral Ecology and Sociobiology* 61(7):1043–1052 (2007).

———. "Intra and Intersexual Selection for Multiple Traits in the Peacock (*Pavo cristatus*)," *Ethology* 111:810–820 (2005).

———. "Non-Defendable Resources Affect Peafowl lek Organization: a Male Removal Experiment," *Behavioural Processes* 74:64–70 (2007).

SCHOLARLY REFERENCE ON FISH PENIS LENGTH AND SEXUAL SELECTION:

Langerhans, R., C. Layman, and T. DeWitt. "Male Genital Size Reflects a Tradeoff Between Attracting Mates and Avoiding Predators in Two Live-bearing Fish Species," *Proceedings of the National Academy of Sciences* 102(21):7618–7623 (2005).

SCHOLARLY REFERENCES ON HUMAN SEXUAL ORNAMENTATION AND MATE CHOICE:

Nettle, D., and H. Clegg. "Schizotypy, Creativity and Mating Success in Humans," *Proceedings of the Royal Society of London* B 273:611–615 (2006).

Kurzban, R., and J. Weeden. "HurryDate: Mate Preferences in Action," *Evolution and Human Behavior* 26(3):227–244 (2005).

SEVERAL POPULAR BOOKS I USED FOR REFERENCE IN DISCUSSING SEXUAL SELECTION AND HUMAN EVOLUTION:

Diamond, Jared. *Why Is Sex Fun?* (Basic Books, 1997).

Klein, Richard. *The Dawn of Human Culture* (Wiley, 2002).

de Waal, Frans. *Our Inner Ape* (Riverhead Books, 2005).

11. ALPHA AND BETA

Parker, Ian. "Swingers: Bonobos Are Celebrated as Peace-loving, Matriarchal and Sexually Liberated. Are They?" *The New Yorker* (July 30, 2007).

SCHOLARLY REFERENCES ON ALPHA MALES:

Sinervo, B., and C. Lively. "The Rock-Paper-Scissors Game and the Evolution of Alternative Male Strategies," *Nature* 380:240–243 (1996).

Sinervo, B., and J. Clobert. "Morphs, Dispersal, Genetic Similarity and the Evolution of Cooperation," *Science* 300:1949–1951 (1996).

Sinervo, B., et al. "Self-Recognition, Color Signals, and Cycles of Greenbeard Mutualism and Altruism," *Proceedings of the National Academy of Sciences* 103(19):7372–7377 (May 9, 2006).

SCHOLARLY REFERENCE ON RECORD-SETTING MALE/FEMALE SIZE DIFFERENCE:

Pietsch, T. "Dimorphism, Parasitism, and Sex Revisited: Modes of Reproduction among Deep-Sea Ceratioid Anglerfishes (Teleostei: Lophiiformes)," *Ichthyology Research* 52:207–236 (2005).

12. WHO'S YOUR DADDY?

SCHOLARLY REFERENCES ON PATERNAL BEHAVIOR
AND MONOGAMY IN ANIMALS:

Lim, M., et al. "Enhanced Partner Preference in a Promiscuous Species by Manipulating the Expression of a Single Gene," *Nature* 429:754–757 (June 17, 2004).

Bales, K., et al. "Effects of Stress on Parental Care are Sexually Dimorphic in Prairie Voles," *Physiology and Behavior* 87:424–429 (2006).

Bales, K., et al. "Effects of Neonatal Oxytocin Manipulations on Male Reproductive Potential in Prairie Voles," *Physiology and Behavior* 81:519–526 (2004).

Bales, K., et al. "Both Oxytocin and Vasopressin May Influence Alloparental Care in Male Prairie Voles," *Hormones and Behavior* 45:354–361 (2004).

Bales, K., L. Pfeifer, and C. Carter. "Sex Differences and Developmental Effects of Manipulations of Oxytocin on Alloparenting and Anxiety in Prairie Voles," *Developmental Psychobiology* 44:123–131 (2004).

Bales, K., and C. Carter. "Sex Differences and Developmental Effects of Oxytocin on Aggression and Social Behavior in Prairie Voles (*Microtus ochrogaster*)," *Hormones and Behavior*, special issue on Aggressive and Violent Behavior, 44:178–184 (2003).

—. "Developmental Exposure to Oxytocin Facilitates Partner Preferences in Male Prairie Voles (*Microtus ochrogaster*)," *Behavioral Neuroscience* 117:854–859 (2003).

Buchan, J., et al. "True Paternal Care in a Multi-Male Primate Society," *Nature* 425:179–181 (Sept. 2003).

SCHOLARLY REFERENCE ON PERCEIVED PARENTAL QUALITIES AND SEXINESS IN HUMANS:

Roney, J., et al. "Reading Men's Faces: Women's Mate Attractiveness Judgments Track Men's Testosterone and Interest in Infants," *Proceedings of the Royal Society of London* B 273:2169–2175 (2006).

IN FISH:

Sabaj, M., J. Armbruster, and L. Page. "Spawning in Ancistrus (Siluriformes: Loricariidae) with Comments on the Evolution of Snout Tentacles as a Novel Reproductive Strategy: Larval Mimicry," *Ichthyological Exploration of Freshwaters* 10(3):217–229 (1999).

13. SEXUAL OUTLAWS

REFERENCES ON INCIDENCE OF HOMOSEXUALITY IN THE POPULATION:

Kinsey, A., W. Pomeroy, and C. Martin. *Sexual Behavior in the Human Male* (W.B. Saunders, 1948).

Kinsey, A., et al. *Sexual Behavior in the Human Female* (W.B. Saunders, 1953).

SOURCE FOR STATISTICS ON LESBIANS:

Kinsey, *Sexual Behavior in the Human Female*, table 142, p. 499.

SOURCE FOR STATISTICS ON MEN WITH ONE HOMOSEXUAL EXPERIENCE:

Kinsey, *Sexual Behavior in the Human Male*, p. 656.

SOURCE FOR INCIDENCE OF MALE HOMOSEXUALITY:

Kinsey, *Sexual Behavior in the Human Male*, p. 651.

A GOOD SOURCE FOR SEXUALITY AND THE ANCIENT WORLD:

Goldhill, Simon. *Love, Sex, and Tragedy: How the Ancient World Shapes Our Lives* (University of Chicago Press, revised edition, 2005).

SCHOLARLY REFERENCES ON HOMOSEXUALITY, THE BRAIN, AND GENETICS:

LeVay, S. "A Difference in Hypothalamic Structure Between Heterosexual and Homosexual Men," *Science* 253:1034–1037 (1991).

Whitman, F., M. Diamond, and J. Martin. "Homosexual Orientation in Twins: A Report on Sixty-one Pairs and Three Triplet Sets," *Archives of Sexual Behavior* 22:187–206 (1993).

King, M., and E. McDonald. "Homosexuals Who Are Twins: A Study of Forty-six Probands," *British Journal of Psychiatry* 160:407–409 (1992).

Eckert, E., et al. "Homosexuality in Monozygotic Twins Reared Apart," *British Journal of Psychiatry* 148:421–425 (1986).

DEAN HAMER'S WORK ON GENETICS:

Hamer, D., et al. "A Linkage between DNA Markers on the X Chromosome and Male Sexual Orientation," *Science* 261:321–327 (1993).

Hu, S., et al. "Linkage between Sexual Orientation and Chromosome Xq28 in Males but Not in Females," *Nature Genetics* 11:248–256 (1995).

SOME FOLLOW-UP STUDIES:

Bailey, J., et al. "A Family History Study of Male Sexual Orientation Using Three Independent Samples," *Behavior and Genetics* 29:79–86 (1999).

Rice, G., et al. "Male Homosexuality: Absence of Linkage to Microsatellite Markers at Xq28," *Science* 284:665–667 (1999).

SCHOLARLY REFERENCES ON MALE BISEXUALITY:

Kinsey, *Sexual Behavior in the Human Male,* table 147, p. 651.

Montgomery, J., et al. "The Extent of Bisexual Behavior in HIV-Infected Men and Implications for Transmission to Their Female Partners," *AIDS Care* 15:829–837 (2003).

Chivers, M., et al. "A Sex Difference in the Specificity of Sexual Arousal," *Psychological Science* 15:736–744 (2004).

Rieger, G., M. Chivers, and J. M. Bailey. "Sexual Arousal Patterns of Bisexual Men," *Psychological Science* 16(8): 579–584 (2005).

SOURCES ON THE DIVERSITY OF MALE SEXUAL BEHAVIOR IN ANIMALS:

Roughgarden, Joan. *Evolution's Rainbow* (University of California Press, 2004). This book offers many intriguing examples of surprising sexual diversity.

Gross, M. "Sneakers, Satellites and Parentals: Polymorphic Mating Strategies in North American Sunfishes," *Zeitschrift fur Tierpsychologie* 60:1–26 (1982).

———. "Evolution of Alternative Reproductive Strategies: Frequency-Dependent Sexual Selection in Male Bluegill Sunfish," *Philosophical Transactions of the Royal Society of London* B 332:59–66 (1991).

Dominey, W. "Female Mimicry in Bluegill Sunfish—a Genetic Polymorphism?" *Nature* 284:546–548 (1980).

SCHOLARLY REFERENCES ON GAY SHEEP RESEARCH:

Bagemihl, Bruce. *Biological Exuberance: Animal Homosexuality and Natural Diversity* (St. Martin's Press, 1999).

Roselli, C., et al. "The Volume of a Sexually Dimorphic Nucleus in the Ovine Medial Preoptic Area / Anterior Hypothalamus Varies with Sexual Partner Preference," *Endocrinology* 145(2):478–483 (Feb. 2004).

SCHOLARLY REFERENCES ON SNAKES, PHEROMONES, AND FEMALE MIMICRY:

Mason, R., and D. Crews. "Female Mimicry As an Alternative Reproductive Tactic in Garter Snakes," *American Zoologist* 23:896 (1983).

Mason, R., et al. "Sex Pheromones in Snakes," *Science* 245:290–293 (1989).

Mason, R., et al. "Characterization, Synthesis, and Behavioral Responses to the Sex Attractiveness Pheromones of Red-Sided Garter Snakes (*Thamnophis sirtalis parietalis*)," *Journal of Chemical Ecology* 16:2353–2369 (1990).

Mason, R. "Hormonal and Pheromonal Correlates of Reproductive Behavior in Garter Snakes," in *Perspectives in Comparative Endocrinology*, edited by K. Davies (Research Journals Division of the National Research Council of Canada, Ottawa, 1994).

Shine, R., et al. "Advantage of Female Mimicry in Snakes," *Nature* 414:267 (2001).

SCHOLARLY REFERENCES ON TRANSSEXUAL FISH:

Black, M., et al. "Reproduction in Context: Field-testing a Lab Model of Socially Controlled Sex Change in Lythrypnus dalli," *Journal of Experimental Marine Biology and Ecology* 318:127–143 (2005).

Black, M., et al. "Socially Induced and Rapid Increases in Aggression Are Inversely Related to Brain Aromatase Activity in a Sex-Changing Fish, Lythrypnus dalli," *Proceedings of the Royal Society of London* B 272:2435–2440 (2005).

Rodgers, E., S. Drane, and M. Grober. "Sex Reversal in Pairs of Lythrypnus dalli: Behavioral and Morphological Changes," *Biological Bulletin* 208: 120–126 (2005).

Drilling, C., and M. Grober. "An Initial Description of Alternative Male Reproductive Tactics in the Bluebanded Goby, Lythrypnus dalli," *Environmental Biology of Fishes* 72:361–372 (2005).

Seruto, C., Y. Sapozhnikova, and D. Schlenk. "Evaluation of the Relationships between Biochemical Endpoints of PAH Exposure and Physiological Endpoints of Reproduction in Male California Halibut (*Paralichthys californicus*) Exposed to Sediments from a Natural Oil Seep," *Marine Environmental Research* 69:454–465 (2005).

14. WHY MALES ARE NECESSARY

Dowd, Maureen. *Are Men Necessary?: When Sexes Collide* (Berkley Trade, 2006). A varied collection of complaints about men.

Adovasio, James, Olga Soffer, and Jake Page. *The Invisible Sex: Uncovering the True Roles of Women in Prehistory* (Collins, 2007). Myth-busting view of prehistory in which women do more than get dragged by the hair and make babies.

Miller, Geoffrey. *The Mating Mind* (Vintage, 2001). Miller examines an intriguing premise that sexual display drove much of evolution and still underlies much of our behavior. I looked at everything from beauty pageants to charitable donations differently after reading this book.

Hrdy, Sarah Blaffer. *Mother Nature: A History of Mothers, Infants, and Natural Selection* (Pantheon, 1999).

FOR MORE ON THE IMPORTANCE OF SEX AND MALES TO OUR SURVIVAL:

Azevedo, R., et al. "Sexual Reproduction Selects for Robustness and Negative Epistasis in Artificial Gene Networks," *Nature* 440:87–90 (2006).

Pennisi, E. "Sex and the Single Killifish," *Science,* News Focus, 313(5792):1381 (Sept. 8, 2006).

INDEX